# Footpath Touring

## with Ken Ward

£1·49  32

# The Best of Lakeland

... 'tis the sense,
Of majesty, and beauty, and repose.
A blended holiness of earth and sky.

William Wordsworth

*Home at Grasmere*

Jarrold Colour Publications, Norwich

# All about Footpath-Touring

This Footpath-Touring guide is designed to lead you easily along a walk which will show you some of the treasures of the Lake District.

**The route:** The route has been divided into daily stages well within the capabilities of those quite new to walking. More experienced walkers, are, of course, free to extend these stages as they wish.

**Getting there:** Full details of public transport and car-parking facilities are given on page 6.

**Accommodation:** Green information panels included on the maps contain advice on overnight accommodation. Unless mentioned, all will provide an evening meal. All have become known to me during my time of walking and research for this guide. I offer them in good faith, without accepting responsibility for them.

Those places where I received a particularly warm welcome are surrounded by a box.

The accommodation is divided into three price categories: economy, medium and not-cheap. All provide reasonable value while some can be outstandingly good. I suggest you always check costs when making reservations, and remember to check that VAT is included.

Where possible the exact locations of accommodation are indicated, however telephone numbers are given should directions be required.

Out of season it should be sufficient to make telephone reservations the day before. This gives you great flexibility in your programme allowing you to take non-walking days to suit inclinations and weather. In high holiday seasons reservations should be made as early as possible. (For non-walking days see page 4.) We recommend that you make it quite clear if an evening meal is required, and, if possible, give some indication of time of arrival.

Please mention Footpath-Touring when booking as all accommodations have been asked to suggest an alternative should they be fully booked.

All accommodations have been selected for their appreciation of the needs of Footpath-Touring walkers particularly regarding warm rooms, good food, drying facilities, early starts and packed lunches.

Where the accommodation is a pub or a licensed establishment this is indicated.

Two letters after the name show the period that accommodation is available, for example, A/O=April to October, M/N=March to November. Those open all year are identified with an □; however, remember that during winter months they may be decorating, taking holidays, or repairing burst water-pipes!

**What you will need:** Remember that you will be carrying your baggage on your back so keep it light!

You will need clothes to walk in, boots, waterproofs, clothes for the evenings, night-wear, toiletries, and little more. These are dealt with below.

**Clothes to walk in:** There is no need to ever be uncomfortable when walking. If you are sweating or are cold you are doing something wrong. Consider your clothing as a layer insulating system that is capable of being added to or decreased as conditions demand. Great flexibility is possible by using layers of thin garments rather than a few thick items. Wherever possible make use of shirts and woollens that button down the front. These are easy to put on and take off, and give a subtle degree of control by using the buttons. Natural fibres like wool and cotton are to be preferred.

Outdoors shops stock special walking trousers or breeches but good-quality trousers purchased anywhere can be equally useful. Jeans are useless. Despite their outdoor image they trap no heat and once wet take a long time to dry. Ladies will probably find trousers more practical than skirts.

With our uncertain climate, gloves can be just as useful in flaming June as in December. Remember, too, that the head is responsible for a very large

# All about Footpath-Touring

heat loss and a woollen hat or Balaclava helmet can provide a great deal of comfort.

A windproof jacket of tight-weave material is essential. This should be front opening, with plenty of pockets, and preferably have a hood.

**Boots:** I consider it essential to wear boots when Footpath-Touring in the Lake District. Many of the paths are very stony and steep. Boots will give the necessary support to your ankles and cushion the soles of your feet. Heed the advice of your local reputable outdoors shop, and select comfortable, lightweight walking boots. And wear them as much as possible before you begin Footpath-Touring. These boots are your wheels and you carry no spare. Choose wisely.

**Waterproofs:** I have walked in the Lake District for periods of up to two weeks in dry weather. However, assume that during your tour there most certainly will be wet days. Rain is no hardship if you are properly protected.

You will need a lightweight waterproof jacket with hood, pockets and front opening. Lightweight waterproof over-trousers that can be slipped over booted feet are also essential. You are strongly advised to equip yourself with lightweight gaiters that go from boot to knee, and I recommend you wear them on all but the driest days. Even when there is no rain they will prevent trouser bottoms from getting wet and heavy from long, dew-laden grass or Lakeland mud. And when you arrive at that hostelry, a flick of the wrist and you could be straight from Savile Row!

**Clothes for the evening:** This is where your ingenuity comes into its own. It is necessary for you to devise a wardrobe that will meet any requirements but will weigh practically nothing. The following check-list may be useful and give you some ideas.

**Ladies:**
- Pullover
- Blouse
- Lightweight crease-resistant trousers or skirt
- Lightweight crease-resistant jacket
- Coloured scarves to provide some variety
- Underclothes
- Light shoes
- Night-wear
- Handkerchiefs
- Toiletries

Remember that you will be staying at a different address every night and any variety is to please only yourself or your Footpath-Touring companions!

**Men:**
- Shirt
- Pullover
- Lightweight crease-resistant trousers
- Lightweight crease-resistant jacket (a safari suit is ideal)
- Tie
- Underclothes
- Socks
- Night-wear
- Handkerchiefs
- Toiletries

*But do keep it light!*

It is possible to buy lightweight haversacks which pack to the size of a lady's purse. These are ideal for packing evening-wear inside your main pack. And they also provide a useful carrier should you wish to walk any time without your main pack. (See 'Non-baggage-carrying days'; page 4.)

**Toiletries:** Your normal toiletries and make-up kit should not weigh more than 9 ounces *255 g*. This can easily be achieved by searching for the smallest packs and refusing to carry glass.

# All about Footpath-Touring

Men who normally use an electric razor might consider using disposable razors for the tour, but remember to take the smallest tube of brushless cream, and a styptic pencil.

**Rucksack:** Assemble all the items you plan to take with you and weigh them.

Ideally this total weight should not exceed 11 lb *5 kg* for an adult man. It is absolutely essential that on no account should it weigh more than 12 lb *6 kg*. Ladies should aim for about 2 lb *1 kg* less depending upon build. Keep trimming until this weight limit is achieved.

You will find that you will need a rucksack with a capacity of about 35 litres. Most shops offer a choice of a rucksack with an outside light metal frame, an internal frame, or no frame at all. I strongly recommend the metal frame variety. A padded hip-belt is essential. This, when fitted across the hips (not round the waist), ensures that the load is carried on the pelvis and not from the shoulders. Shoulder-straps should be wide and padded. When buying I suggest you ask the salesman to load the pack and allow you to walk round his shop. It is essential that the pack feels comfortable.

**Water-bottle:** It is sensible to have a small water-bottle with you.

**Lunches:** On most Footpath-Touring routes, the days are arranged so that about midday the walker is near an establishment where refreshments can be obtained. However, this Tour goes every day into the high hills, and packed lunches will usually be required. At the commencement of every day in the guide, notice is given when a packed lunch is necessary.

A small vacuum-flask would be a useful item to have with you for these lunch breaks.

**Non-walking days:** You may walk the whole route in consecutive days. However if you are new to walking you are urged to include some non-walking days. These will enable you to take a late breakfast, explore the area, or merely lick wounds. Grasmere is an ideal place for such a day off. (See page 37.)

If poor weather or other causes suggest taking an unscheduled non-walking day, the next overnight stop can always be joined by taxi.

Any of the taxi-operators detailed on the maps will transport you. Always ask the fare first, and mention Footpath-Touring to get the benefit of any advantageous rates.

**Non-baggage-carrying days:** If the luxury of a non-baggage-carrying day appeals to you then the same taxi-operators will transport your pack during the morning. Again check charges first and mention Footpath-Touring to benefit from reasonable rates. This is where your lightweight haversack, suggested on page 3, will be indispensable for carrying wet gear, camera and snacks.

**Good behaviour:** Many thousands walk in the Lake District every year. Most behave in a responsible and thoughtful manner. Unfortunately a few do not. Please be most careful about reclosing gates, keeping dogs under control, causing no damage and leaving no litter. Please.

**Maps:** The guide maps together with the directions, allow you to easily follow the route. However I suggest that you may wish to equip yourself with the excellent Ordnance Survey tourist map of the Lake District which covers the whole tour and will enable you to identify features seen on horizons.

# This Lakeland Footpath-Touring route

The tour begins with a ride on the narrow-gauge, steam-hauled railway that travels from Ravenglass to Eskdale. This 7 mile *11 km* journey travels right to the foot of the giants of Lakeland and makes a delightful introduction to the pleasures to come.

However I am aware that some hardy walkers may be making the tour during the early months of the year when the little railway offers only a limited service. For these I have included an attractive route which will take them easily to Boot with about 4½ hours' walking.

## How many days?

I have divided the Footpath-Tour into what I think are practical walking days, but the actual length of time you take to complete the whole tour is up to you.

For instance your programme could look like this:

| | |
|---|---|
| First day | Travel to Ravenglass. Catch the 16.35 Ravenglass/Eskdale train arriving at Boot at 17.15 hrs. |
| Second day | Walk from Boot to Wastwater. |
| Third day | Walk from Wastwater to Borrowdale. |
| Fourth day | Walk from Borrowdale to Grasmere. |
| Fifth day | Morning in Grasmere. Visit Wordsworth Museum and Dove Cottage. In afternoon walk to Patterdale. |
| Sixth day | Walk from Patterdale to Troutbeck. Visit NT Townend Farmhouse. |
| Seventh day | Walk from Troutbeck to Windermere (about 3 hours). Catch train home from Windermere. Or travel by bus to pick up car. |

However, there is much to linger over and you are urged to stretch your programme over as many days as you have available. Your tour might even look something like this:

| | |
|---|---|
| First day | Travel to Ravenglass. Visit Muncaster Castle, remains of Roman baths. |
| Second day | By narrow-gauge steam railway to Boot. Visit Stanley Ghyll waterfalls or walk to see dramatic site of Roman fort on Hardknott Pass. |
| Third day | Walk to Wastwater. |
| Fourth day | Walk to Borrowdale. |
| Fifth day | Walk to Grasmere. |
| Sixth day | Spend a non-walking day in Grasmere. Rest, shop or explore. Visit the Wordsworth Museum, Dove Cottage and St Oswald's Church. A 15 minute bus ride will take you to the beautifully situated village of Ambleside. National Trust Information Centre. Doll's House museum. Heritage Centre. Cinema. Some good shops and eating-places. Ribble buses every hour in the summer, every 2 hours in the winter. Inquiries telephone 0539 20932. |
| Seventh day | Walk to Patterdale/Glenridding. |
| Eighth day | Lake 'steamer' to Howtown. Walk by lake path back to Patterdale/Glenridding. |
| Ninth day | Walk over High Street to Troutbeck. Visit NT Townend Farmhouse. |
| Tenth day | Morning walk to Windermere. Visit Steamboat Museum and the National Park Centre at Brockhole. |
| Eleventh day | Catch train home from Windermere. Or travel by bus to pick up car. |

# Getting to Ravenglass

**By rail:** British Rail operates trains to Ravenglass via Carlisle or Barrow-in-Furness, every day but Sunday, throughout the year. Inquiries telephone 01 387 7070.

**By car:** Cars may be parked in the Railway Station yard at Barrow-in-Furness. Trains from Barrow, Monday to Saturday throughout the year, at 13.20 hrs (arrives Ravenglass 14.12 hrs) and 14.54 hrs (arrives Ravenglass 15.46 hrs).
Trains from Ravenglass to Boot see below.
Note that parking at Barrow-in-Furness rather than Ravenglass simplifies returning to the car at the end of Footpath-Touring (see below).

**By coach:** National Express operate coach services to Barrow-in-Furness throughout the year. Inquiries telephone 0229 35008.

## Ravenglass to Boot

Ravenglass & Eskdale Railway (see page 11).
   The journey from Ravenglass to Dalegarth (Boot) takes 45 minutes.
   A limited service operates throughout the year but from the end of May to end of August there are about eight trains a day; twelve a day in August. A free time-table gives all times, including details of steam-hauled services. Send stamped addressed envelope to Ravenglass & Eskdale Railway, Ravenglass, Cumbria CA18 1SW. Telephone 06577 226. Show this Footpath-Touring guide at the ticket office to obtain a special fare concession.
   Note that the last train from Ravenglass to Boot leaves at 16.35 hrs throughout the year.

**Taxi:** William Sim & Son of Boot, operate a taxi service throughout the year. Telephone 094 03 227.

**Time to spare:** If you have time to spare in Ravenglass before you take the Ravenglass & Eskdale train, the 1½ mile *2.5 km* walk past the Roman baths to visit Muncaster Castle (see page 11) is strongly recommended.

## At the end of the Footpath-Tour
## Travel from Windermere

**By rail:** British Rail operates approximately four trains a day throughout the year, from Windermere to Oxenholme to connect with the main-line system.

**By coach:** National Express coaches run from Windermere throughout the year to connect with the countrywide system. Inquiries telephone 0966 33233.

## To return to car parked
## at Barrow-in-Furness

Ribble bus, service 518, departs opposite Windermere Railway Station (see map on page 62), at 11.51 hrs and 13.51 hrs daily, Monday to Saturday throughout the year. Arrives at Barrow-in-Furness Railway Station at 13.27 hrs and 15.27 hrs. Inquiries telephone 0539 20932.

# Walking in Lakeland

These wonderful mountains offer superb walking, a sense of well being and great freedom. However they expect to be taken seriously. They demand that walkers be properly dressed and shod. They require that those wandering off indicated routes should be experienced in navigation. And these mountains can play impressive tricks with the weather. A fine sunny morning can develop into something most hostile within the hour. However, all the Footpath-Touring day stages are short, so that if the weather does begin to look ominous you can be off the mountain in quite a short time. Take the precaution of making daily use of the excellent Lake District weather forecast service, see inside back cover. Treat the mountains with respect and they will reward you richly.

# Ravenglass

Ravenglass sits on the Cumbrian coast where three rivers, the Esk, the Mite, and the Irt meander into the sea.

In 79 BC, the Romans, under Julius Agricole, established an important harbour here. Apart from being the Romans' major harbour on the north-west coast, the adjoining Fort of Glannaventa was the southern terminus of the line of coastal forts which formed part of the Hadrian defence system, of which the coast-to-coast wall is the best-known section. From here the Romans built a road up the Esk Valley, and established another fort beyond Boot, magnificently located below Hardknott Pass. All that now remains of the playing-card plan of Glannaventa Fort, are earth embankments obscured by fir trees, and cut through by the railway engineers. However as at Hardknott, the Romans built a bath house outside the main fort. Probably because a wooden building would not stand up to steam and damp, they invariably built these bath houses of stone. So the wooden walls of the fort have long gone, while the bath house remains. Sound building and tenacious mortar have largely resisted the efforts of stone-stealers ever since, and the 13 feet *4 m* high arches can be seen from the walking route to Boot (see page 11).

The harbour remained in existence after the Romans left. The Angles settled here about AD 700, and the Vikings included it on their list of favourite pillaging points about AD 900.

**Pearl-fishing** In the 16thC there was a flourishing fish curing and exporting industry. In 1695, a local man, intrigued by stories that the Romans used to find pearls here, set up a pearl-fishing organisation, and records insist that he found £800 worth!

In the 18thC, Ravenglass was an important shipbuilding centre, and a busy port for cattle-importing. It also is said to have had a busy smuggling industry, running goods of all kinds from the Isle of Man (about 30 miles to the West) which had no excise.

The present day one-street hamlet gives little indication of its past busy history.

**10,000 pairs of Black-headed Gulls** The largest colony of Black-headed Gulls in Europe lives on the estuary in the Gullery Nature Reserve. Other birds include several species of Terns. Access is from the Drigg/beach road, about 6 miles. Permits are required: apply Cumbria County Council, Estates and Valuation Department, The Castle, Carlisle CA3 8XF – *Telephone* 0228 23456.

# The route

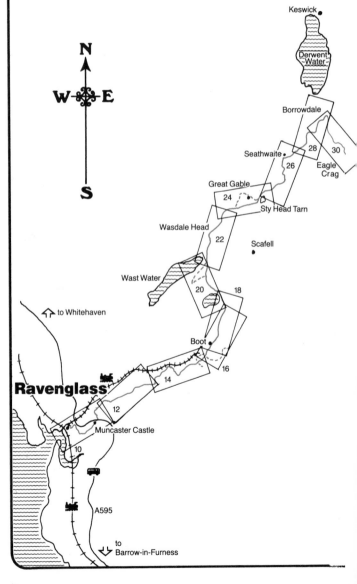

N
W—E
S

Keswick

Derwent Water

Borrowdale

Seathwaite

28

30

26

Eagle Crag

Great Gable

24

Sty Head Tarn

Wasdale Head

22

Scafell

Wast Water

20

18

to Whitehaven

Boot

16

Ravenglass

14

12

Muncaster Castle

10

A595

to Barrow-in-Furness

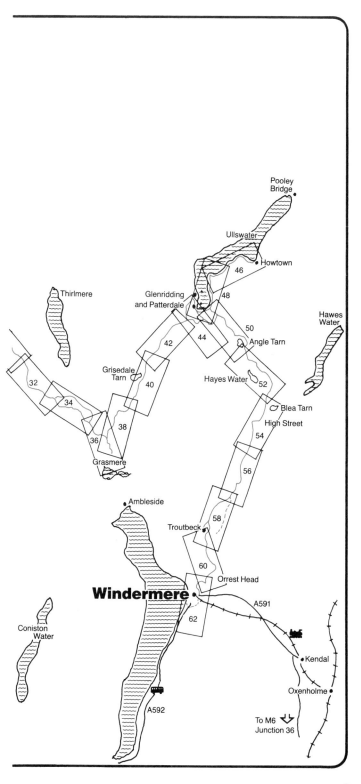

Pooley
Bridge

Ullswater

Howtown

46

48

Thirlmere

Glenridding
and Patterdale

50

Angle Tarn

Hawes
Water

42

44

Grisedale
Tarn

Hayes Water

52

32

40

Blea Tarn

34

High Street

38

54

36

Grasmere

56

Ambleside

58

Troutbeck

60

Orrest Head

**Windermere**

A591

62

Coniston
Water

Kendal

Oxenholme

A592

To M6
Junction 36

9

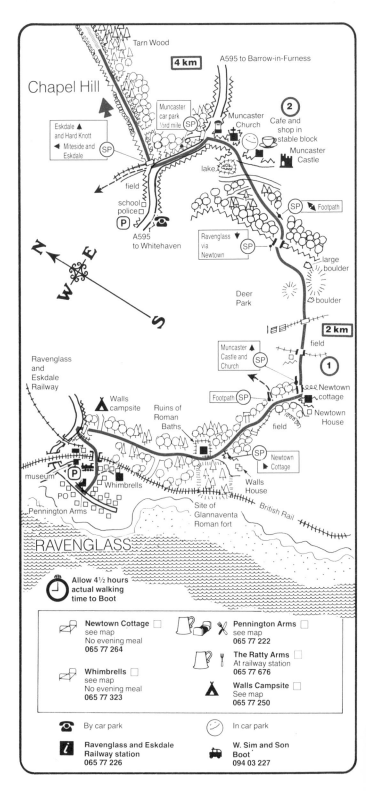

Tarn Wood

A595 to Barrow-in-Furness

**4 km**

Chapel Hill

Muncaster
car park
½ard mile  SP

Muncaster Church

**②**

Cafe and
shop in
stable block

Eskdale ▲
and Hard Knott

◀ Miteside and
Eskdale  SP

Muncaster
Castle

lake

field

SP  ◤ Footpath

school ☐
police ☐

**P**

☎

A595
to Whitehaven

Ravenglass ▼
via
Newtown  SP

large
boulder

☼ boulder

Deer
Park

N
W  E
S

**2 km**

field

Muncaster ▲
Castle and
Church  SP

**①**

Ravenglass
and
Eskdale
Railway

Walls
campsite

Ruins of
Roman
Baths

Footpath  SP

Newtown
cottage

☐ Newtown
House

field

SP  Newtown
▶ Cottage

museum

**P**

Whimbrells

PO

Pennington Arms

Walls
House

Site of
Glannaventa
Roman fort

British Rail

RAVENGLASS

🕐 Allow 4½ hours
actual walking
time to Boot

🛏 **Newtown Cottage** ☐
see map
No evening meal
065 77 264

🫖✕ **Pennington Arms** ☐
see map
065 77 222

🛏 **Whimbrells** ☐
see map
No evening meal
065 77 323

🫖🍴 **The Ratty Arms** ☐
At railway station
065 77 676

⛺ **Walls Campsite** ☐
See map
065 77 250

☎ By car park

⊘ In car park

ℹ **Ravenglass and Eskdale
Railway station**
065 77 226

🚒 **W. Sim and Son
Boot**
094 03 227

Ravenglass to Boot 1
Lunch: Depending upon your time schedule, either the Stables
Café at Muncaster Castle (below), or the King George IV pub
(page 15) should well satisfy your needs.

## Ravenglass to Chapel Hill

See notes on page 6 about getting to Ravenglass.
**Going**: This walk is an alternative to the delightful, 7 mile *11 km*
journey by narrow-gauge steam railway from Ravenglass to Boot
(see page 5).
   An easy woodland and field walk leads to the grounds of
Muncaster Castle, followed by a climb up a hedge-enclosed lane.

**Leave the British Rail station by the footbridge.**
On the left are the buildings of the Ravenglass & Eskdale Railway,
known to Cumbrians as 'T'laal Ratty' (The little Ratty) after Mr
Ratcliffe, the Engineer who built the line. It was opened in 1875 to
carry iron ore from Eskdale. The group of station buildings include
a pub, The Ratty Arms; a shop; and a fascinating museum telling
the story of the railway.

**Continue from footbridge through children's playground.
Emerge at road and immediately turn Right up private tree-lined
drive. Wall Campsite on Left. In 5 minutes arrive at remains of
Roman bath house on Left (see page 7).**
In fir trees on Right, earth banks are all that remain of Glannaventa
Fort.

**Take Left Fork, signposted Newtown Cottage, where drive
goes Right to Walls House. Again in about 3 minutes take Left fork
also signposted Newtown Cottage.**

**Opposite Newtown Cottage, cross stile and follow track
through rough ground. Over stile into field. Bear very slightly Right
to pass through gate in fence that is seen as slope is climbed.**

**Keep high point of field Right, and head for wall enclosing
trees of Muncaster Castle. Cross stile into castle grounds. The
right-of-way path through the grounds is well maintained and
signposted. Keep to this path.**
The magnificent gardens of Muncaster Castle are famous
throughout Europe. The right-of-way passes through
rhododendrons, azaleas, camellias and bamboos. By the path is a
fenced pond on which are kept exotic birds. In the stables are an
interesting shop and pleasant café, open 12.00 to 17.00 hrs every
day but Monday, Easter to October.
   If you desire to wander off the through-path to further explore
the famous gardens then you must pay at the shop.
   To see the house and its many treasures, open Tuesdays,
Wednesdays, Thursdays and Sundays from 14.00 to 17.00 hrs, also
pay at the shop.

**Continue on drive, past stable block.**
Beyond the stables, in a ring of trees on the Right, is the Church of
St Michael and All Angels. Inside is a magnificently carved font.

**At North Lodge emerge on to busy A595 road, cross and
turn Left. As road makes sharp bend to Left enter Fell Lane on
Right for steep climb to Chapel Hill.**
There are fine views of the estuary from the lane. To the West, 30
miles out in the Irish Sea, lies the Isle of Man.

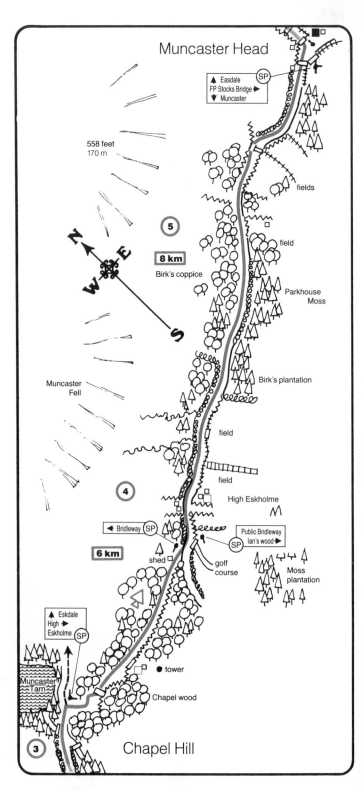

# Muncaster Head

Easdale ▲
FP Stocks Bridge ►
Muncaster ▼

558 feet
170 m

⑤

**8 km**

Birk's coppice

fields

field

Parkhouse Moss

Birk's plantation

Muncaster Fell

field

field

④

High Eskholme

◄ Bridleway SP

Public Bridleway
Ian's wood ►

**6 km**

shed

golf course

Moss plantation

▲ Eskdale
High ► Eskholme
SP

● tower

Muncaster Tarn

Chapel wood

③

# Chapel Hill

# Chapel Hill to Muncaster Head

**Going:** A downhill path through bracken, emerges on to a tarmac lane. Very easy going.

**The steepness of Fell Lane eases off at trees on the Left where a track leads to Muncaster Tarn.**

The attractive tarn, surrounded by trees, was built by Lord Muncaster years ago in an area of swamp. It is no longer part of the Muncaster Estate and is private!

**Just beyond the entrance to the tarn, a narrow green lane leads off to the Right, signposted High Eskholme.**

This lane and the preceding Fell Lane, is thought to be the route of the Roman road from Glannaventa Fort to Mediobogdum Fort on Hardknott Pass, and onward to Brocavum Fort, near Brougham at Penrith.

In places the path is pleasantly terraced giving fine views over the Esk Valley.

**Continue down through bracken and bushes, with a wall running more or less parallel on the Right.**

By farm buildings, just below the path on the Right, is a strange-looking round tower. This folly was built about 1800 by Lord Muncaster to mark the spot where, in 1464, shepherds found a weary and much-stained King Henry VI, fleeing from his defeat during the Wars of the Roses. The shepherds guided him to Muncaster Castle where Sir John Pennington, then Lord of the Manor, gave him shelter. Eventually the fugitive King set forth, only to be betrayed by a monk in Lancashire, and to be incarcerated in the Tower of London where seven years later he met a violent death. To mark his appreciation of the refuge, the King presented the Penningtons with an enamelled glass bowl which the family still own. This priceless object is known as the 'Luck of Muncaster'. It is not recorded whether the shepherds received any award. No such luck for them!

**Continue descending until a tarmac lane is reached. Turn Left. Golf-course on Right.**

On Right of lane, beyond High Eskholme, archaeologists have identified a Roman tile and pottery kiln. However it is not marked and I have never been able to find it.

Across the valley lies Birkby Fell. Groups of stone at Barnscar are thought to mark the site of a Viking settlement.

The tree-covered slopes of Muncaster Fell on the Left are said to be haunted by the distraught figure of a woman cradling the dismembered head of her lover. The story goes that the girl's father had the head removed to discourage the would-be lover. Not all that subtle!

**At Muncaster Head farm turn Left through the farmyard.**

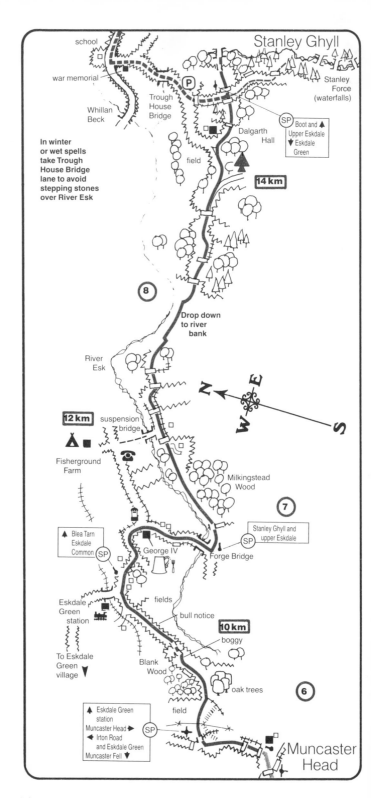

Stanley Ghyll

school

war memorial

Whillan Beck

Trough House Bridge

P

Stanley Force (waterfalls)

SP Boot and ▲ Upper Eskdale ▼ Eskdale Green

Dalgarth Hall

field

**In winter or wet spells take Trough House Bridge lane to avoid stepping stones over River Esk**

14 km

8

Drop down to river bank

River Esk

12 km

▲ ■

suspension bridge

Fisherground Farm

☎

Milkingstead Wood

7

SP Stanley Ghyll and upper Eskdale

▲ Blea Tarn Eskdale Common SP

George IV

Forge Bridge

Eskdale Green station

fields

bull notice

To Eskdale Green village ▼

10 km

boggy

Blank Wood

oak trees

6

field

▲ Eskdale Green station
Muncaster Head ►
◄ Irton Road and Eskdale Green
Muncaster Fell ▼
SP

Muncaster Head

# Muncaster Head to Stanley Ghyll

**Going**: A sometimes muddy lane walk leads to Esk Valley road and a pub. This is followed by a pleasant river walk to Dalegarth Hall.

Leave Muncaster Head farmyard by gate and follow wall on Left. At gate across track, turn Right to walk across field along top of depression. Head for corner of wall enclosing saplings, and pass beneath oak-topped knoll on Right. Follow wall on Left down to gorse-filled hollow. By boggy patch cross two stiles and stepping-stones, to enter narrow walled lane. Emerge on to busy road by Eskdale Green Station of the Ravenglass & Eskdale Railway.

Turn Right on road. In 5 minutes arrive at the King George IV pub.

This popular pub was called the King of Prussia until the brewery bowed to patriotic fervour during the First World War.

At pub take Right fork to cross Forge Bridge over the River Esk. Immediately over bridge turn Left and follow good track that enters Milkingstead Wood and closely follows the River Esk.

Suspension bridge on Left leads to Fisherground Farm Campsite. Telephone is on road.

Continue on easily followed track through pastures and woods. Watch for point where path drops down to river edge for a few yards, before climbing back up to gate to enter Dalegarth Wood.

At wall surrounding Dalegarth Hall bear Right.

Dalegarth Hall, with its distinctive round chimneys, dates from the 15thC.

Past crags on Left and through gate to emerge on to a stony track. Cross stony track to field gate opposite. Important. The route ahead involves crossing the River Esk by stepping-stones. These are quite safe during the summer months but during the winter, or in particularly wet spells, these stepping-stones will be impassable. In these conditions turn Left down the stony track to reach the Esk Valley road, by the War Memorial. Turn Right up the road to Boot.

If time permits turn Right up track to see the Stanley Ghyll waterfalls. The falls are only about 60 feet *18 m* high but their situation among fir trees and ferns is most spectacular. Where track bends to Right go through gate on left to enter Stanley Ghyll Access Area. Three footbridges, the joint efforts of the Cumberland County Council and the Eskdale Green Outward Bound Mountain School, cross and recross the stream, the third bridge giving easy viewing of the falls. The path continues upward but gets progressively more rugged. When you have seen enough, retrace your steps to rejoin the main route at crossing of stony track.

From stony track, cross field. In trees, cross Stanley Ghyll by footbridge.

Penny Hill Farm Ea/O
No evening meal
see map
094 03 274

Woolpack Inn ☐
see map
094 03 230

Burnmoor Inn ☐
see map
094 03 224

Hollins Farm ☐
see map
094 03 253

Brook House Hotel J/N
see map
094 03 288

YH  Eskdale Youth Hostel J/N
see map
094 03 219

☎ see map

⌣ In station car park
see map

🚗 W. Sim and Son
Boot
094 03 227

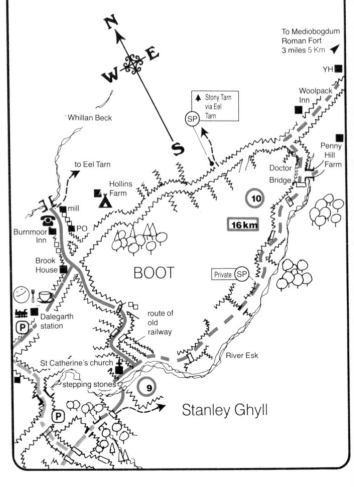

# Stanley Ghyll to Boot

**Going**: Across the River Esk by stepping-stones and a short walk up into the hamlet of Boot. Or a slightly longer, but easily followed, riverside path to the Woolpack Inn, the YHA Hostel and Penny Hill farm.

**From Stanley Ghyll Footbridge up to wall and through to field. Bear Left to wicket-gate and stepping-stones over River Esk. (See note on page 15 about high water.)**

**Over stepping-stones to St Catherine's Church.**

There has been a church here for 600 years. The Priory of St Bees was founded in 1125 and here in Eskdale it built one of four dale chapels. The others were in Ennerdale, Wasdale and Loweswater. However for baptisms and burials, the dales people were obliged to make the long journey of almost 20 miles to St Bees. In 1445 they petitioned the Pope, and the chapel was upgraded to parish church. This upgrading meant that the churchyard now became the burial ground for both Eskdale and Wasdale. Our route tomorrow follows the old Corpse Road over which coffins were carried from Wasdale by cart or on horseback.

In 1881 the church was virtually rebuilt. The octagonal font is carved with St Catherine's wheel and ancient marigold designs. It was rescued in 1876 from the farm, just up the lane, where it had been used for 60 years 'for vile purposes'.

Some of the tombstones are of interest, including one suitably decorated to mark the last resting-place of a well-known local huntsman.

The small sandstone cross on the east end gable is thought to date from the original chapel.

**Walk up walled lane. At gate take Right fork.**

**In a few yards, at sharp Right bend, observe gates on opposite sides of lane. These two gates mark the route of a branch line of the Ravenglass & Eskdale Railway, (see below).**

**Continue up lane to cross Esk Valley road into Boot hamlet.**

**For those intending to stay at the Woolpack Inn or the Eskdale Youth Hostel, there is an attractive, easy to follow river walk to Doctor's Bridge, then by lane up to the Esk Valley road and turn Right.**

Dalegarth Station is the present Eskdale terminus of the Ravenglass & Eskdale Railway.

The original line by-passed Dalegarth on its way up to Boot to serve the Nab Gill iron-ore mines. A few years later a branch line was established from Beckfoot to serve the Gill Force Mines down on the south side of the River Esk. Dalegarth was on this branch line. In 1912 the Nab Gill Mines were flooded out of operation and the line closed. In 1915, Mr W. J. Bassett-Lowke, a famous model railway engineer, purchased the line to test his 15-inch-gauge model steam locomotives. The incline up to Boot proved to be too severe and so the line was eventually terminated at Dalegarth.

The present station contains a shop and a refreshment room.

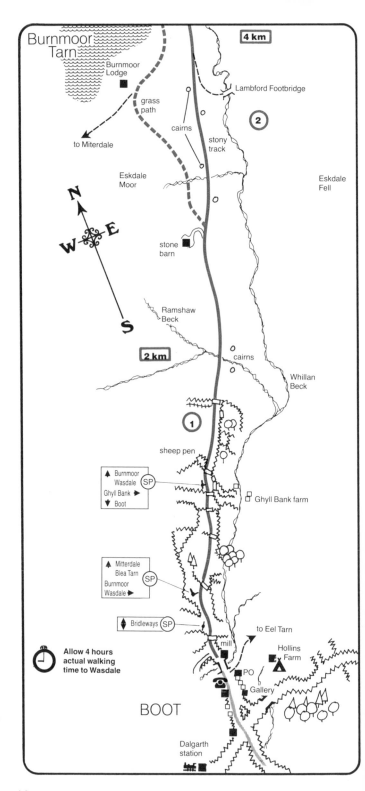

Burnmoor Tarn

Burnmoor Lodge

grass path

to Miterdale

cairns

stony track

**4 km**

Lambford Footbridge

**②**

Eskdale Moor

Eskdale Fell

N

W   E

S

stone barn

Ramshaw Beck

**2 km**

cairns

Whillan Beck

**①**

sheep pen

▲ Burnmoor Wasdale
Ghyll Bank ►
▼ Boot   SP

Ghyll Bank farm

▲ Mitterdale Blea Tarn
Burnmoor Wasdale ►   SP

Bridleways   SP

to Eel Tarn

mill

Hollins Farm

PO

Gallery

🕐 Allow 4 hours actual walking time to Wasdale

BOOT

Dalgarth station

Boot to Wasdale 1
Lunch: Today's walk passes no refreshment places so a packed
lunch will be necessary.

# Boot to Burnmoor Tarn

**Going**: An easy walk through wall-enclosed pastures, followed by
an easily followed track over wild Eskdale Moor.

Boot is a pleasant little hamlet superbly situated in the beautiful
Esk Valley. Accommodation is limited. There are two hotels and an
inn well known to walkers for many years. There is also a youth
hostel and a campsite. The Fold End Gallery located in a loft is
worth a visit; you won't be badgered to buy. There is also a Post
Office-cum-general shop, and a preserved Corn Mill (see below).

Three miles *5 km* up the road to the Hardknott Pass is the site of
the Roman Fort of Mediobogdum. It was built about AD 100 and
was garrisoned by troops from Yugoslavia. The layout of the
standard Roman Fort is well demonstrated. Sections of the walls
have been restored to their original height. Outside the fort is the
parade ground, with platform, where the salute was taken and
orders given. A spectacularly positioned defence work standing at
over 800 feet *240 m*.

**Leave Boot over a 17thC pack-horse bridge by a restored
Corn Mill.**

The name of the Woolpack Inn on the valley road is a reminder of
the pack-horse trains of the wool merchants, that came this way on
the long journey from Kendal to the port of Whitehaven.

The Corn Mill has been restored to working order by the
Cumbrian County Council. Power is provided by a 12 feet *4 m*
diameter 'overshot' wheel. In addition there is a second 'undershot'
wheel. A small exhibition features the history and techniques of
milling. If you arrive in Boot in time I think you will enjoy looking
in at this piece of Eskdale history. There has been a mill here for
over 300 years. Opens every day except Saturday, 11.00 to 17.00
hrs, Easter to September. Admission 50p.

**Bear Right between walls up to a gate on the Right,
signposted to Burnmoor and Wasdale.**

**The path is easily followed through a series of gates. The
last gate opens out on to Eskdale Moor.**

This is the old Corpse Road between Wasdale and Eskdale (see
page 17).

**Just over 200 yards *183 m* from the gate, cross Ramshaw
Beck. Stone cairns mark the track from here.**

About ½ mile *0.8 km* away to the Left, on the empty moor, is a series
of stone circles, enclosing stone-lined pits, that contain the
remains of human cremations believed to have been carried out
over 3000 years ago.

**At a stone barn, an alternative track to the Left heads for
Burnmoor Lodge, before rejoining by the tarn. Slightly longer and
not marked by cairns, but certainly less stony.**

Burnmoor Tarn is the property of the National Trust who give you
permission to fish here for the trout, if you so desire!

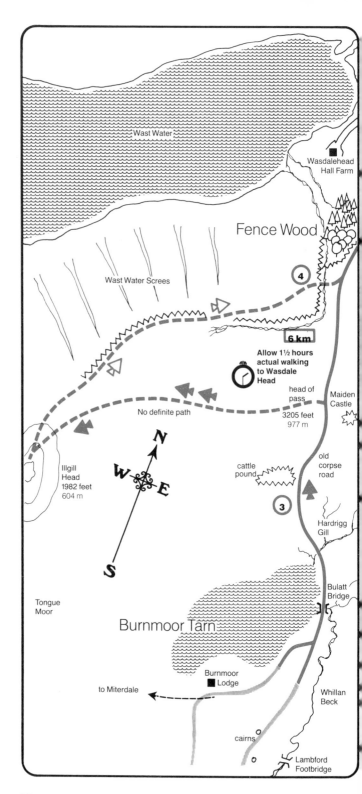

Wast Water

Wasdalehead Hall Farm

Fence Wood

Wast Water Screes

**4**

**6 km**

**Allow 1½ hours actual walking to Wasdale Head**

head of pass
3205 feet
977 m

Maiden Castle

No definite path

N
W E
S

Illgill Head
1982 feet
604 m

cattle pound

old corpse road

**3**

Hardrigg Gill

Tongue Moor

Bulatt Bridge

Burnmoor Tarn

Whillan Beck

Burnmoor Lodge

to Miterdale

cairns

Lambford Footbridge

# Burnmoor Tarn to Fence Wood

**Going:** The pleasant, sometimes soggy track leaves the tarn to rise steadily over the wild moor to the head of the pass at 977 feet *290 m*. From here the track descends gently to Fence Wood.

**Cross Bulatt Bridge in the rather wet area by the tarn, and climb to pass by a walled cattle pound ahead.**

As you leave the tarn it is interesting to note that the main feeding stream of Hardrigg Gill enters the tarn at almost the same place as the exit stream of Whillan Beck. When there is a great deal of water about, some of it takes a crafty short cut, avoiding the tarn altogether.

There is a local legend concerning a funeral party that was escorting the body of a young man along this Corpse Road from Wasdale. Near Burnmoor Tarn the pony carrying the coffin suddenly reared with fright, bolted over the fell, and was lost. The shock of this resulted within a few days in the death of the distraught mother. Strange to tell, at the exact spot of the previous tragedy, the horse carrying her coffin also reared and bolted. A search-party failed to find the horse but came upon the pony lost earlier with the body of the son, and the burial took place in Eskdale. The horse carrying the mother's body was never found. There have since been strange stories that lone travellers, walking near Burnmoor Tarn in heavy mist, have been startled by a horse that thundered by, nostrils flared, black mane flowing, and bearing on its back a coffin-shaped box!

**At the summit of the pass, on the Right, just off the track, is Maiden Castle.**

This Maiden Castle in no way resembles the magnificent earthwork fortification in Dorset, being merely a small, stone-walled circular enclosure. However, it makes a useful shelter in which to take a rest when wind and rain lash over the pass.

A diversion can be made from here up the steep grass slopes on the Left to Illgill Head. A cairn marks this high point of the screes that tumble down to Wastwater and there are superb views over the 3 mile *4·8 km* long lake which lies almost 2000 feet *600 m* directly below. However, it is a steep pull up of over almost 1000 feet *300 m* so let your decision be guided by the weather, your watch and your walking legs. A track follows the remains of a wall down to Fence Wood where you may rejoin the main route.

**As the path descends towards Fence Wood there are ever-developing views of magnificent Wastwater. Depending upon your time schedule, anywhere here would seem to offer an ideal place to take an early lunch, and lie back to enjoy the splendour of your surroundings.**

The great bulk immediately ahead across the valley is Yewbarrow of 2058 feet *636 m*.

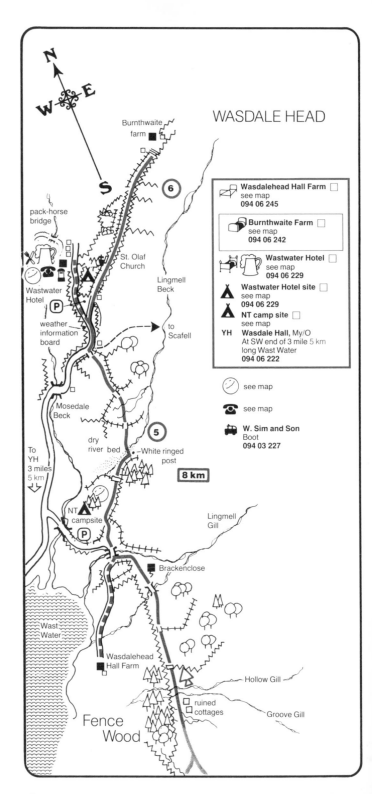

WASDALE HEAD

Burnthwaite farm ■

6

pack-horse bridge

St. Olaf Church

Lingmell Beck

Wastwater Hotel

P

weather information board

to Scafell

Mosedale Beck

dry river bed

5

White ringed post

8 km

Lingmell Gill

To YH 3 miles 5 km

NT campsite

P

Brackenclose

Wast Water

Wasdalehead Hall Farm

Hollow Gill

ruined cottages

Groove Gill

Fence Wood

| | Wasdalehead Hall Farm ☐ see map 094 06 245 |
| --- | --- |
| | Burnthwaite Farm ☐ see map 094 06 242 |
| | Wastwater Hotel ☐ see map 094 06 229 |
| ▲ | Wastwater Hotel site ☐ see map 094 06 229 |
| ▲ | NT camp site ☐ see map |
| YH | Wasdale Hall, My/O At SW end of 3 mile 5 km long Wast Water 094 06 222 |

⊘ see map

☎ see map

🚐 W. Sim and Son Boot 094 03 227

# Fence Wood to Wasdale Head

**Going:** Easily down into Wasdale followed by a pleasant level walk along the floor of the valley to Wasdale Head, lying in the shadows of some of Lakeland's giants.

A stony track drops down with Fence Wood and wall on the Left, and remains of cottages on the Right.

Cross over Groove Gill and Hollow Gill.

After Brackenclose, the lodge of the Fell and Rock Climbing Club, cross bridge over Lingmell Gill and follow to Right a Bridlepath sign to Wasdale Head, through National Trust campsite. (Toilets in copse at centre of site.)

Leave campsite at gate by small fir-tree plantation. After few yards, at wooden post with white marking, turn Left across stony, dry river-bed to obvious track disappearing through bushes opposite.

During very wet periods the path may suffer flooding, in which case return to campsite and cross bridge over Lingmell Beck and walk up by road.

Follow well-maintained track (you are in the efficient hands of the National Trust) to join the road. Turn Right on road to Wasdale Head.

Over on the Right are the magnificent slopes of Sca Fell 3162 feet *964 m* and Scafell Pike, 3210 feet *978 m*, England's highest mountain.

Farther up the valley, on the Right, is Lingmell 2649 feet *807 m.*

At car park fork Left for Wastwater Hotel, and fork Right, along walled lane, for Burnthwaite farm.

The farm stands at the foot of Kirk Fell, 2631 feet *802 m.* To the right of that is the pyramid of Great Gable, 2949 feet *899m*, for many the symbol of Lakeland.

The hotel has a bar that welcomes walkers and offers some good, well-kept beers. The Barn Door outdoor equipment shop in the hotel courtyard has everything a Footpath-Tourer might need, or might have forgotten to pack, and staff are able to offer good, experienced advice.

Behind the hotel is a well-preserved example of a pack-horse bridge, narrow and low sided to allow the passage of ponies laden with bulky loads.

Along the walled lane to Burnthwaite, half hidden in a clump of yew trees, is the tiny Church of St Olaf, one of England's many 'smallest' churches. Outside in the tiny churchyard are several melancholy stones in memory of deaths on the surrounding mountains, and in the Himalayas. If possible try to find time for a few quiet minutes in this area of sanctuary.

Cumbrians used to joke that Wasdale contained England's deepest lake, its highest mountain, its smallest church, and its biggest liar. The latter was said to be Will Ritson, landlord of the inn, famous for his outrageous stories.

Many generations of walkers and climbers have spent time in this peak-surrounded valley head. Perhaps this accounts for the special atmosphere that is easily detected here; a rare blend of anticipation and excitement, soothed with a touch of tranquillity.

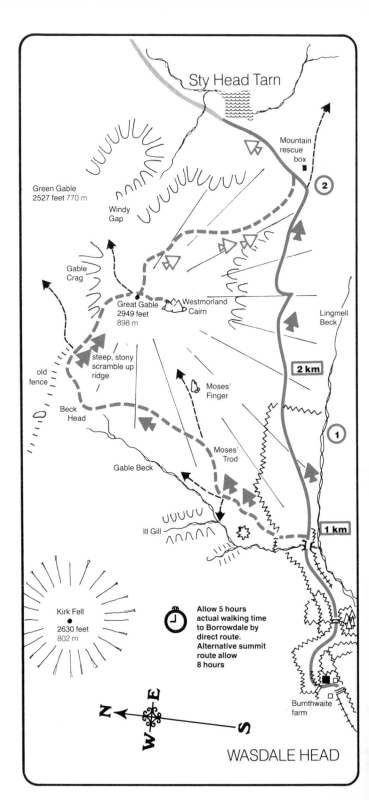

Sty Head Tarn

Mountain
rescue
box

(2)

Green Gable
2527 feet 770 m

Windy
Gap

Gable
Crag

Great Gable
2949 feet
898 m

Westmorland
Cairn

Lingmell
Beck

2 km

steep, stony
scramble up
ridge

old
fence

Moses'
Finger

Beck
Head

(1)

Moses'
Trod

Gable Beck

1 km

Ill Gill

Kirk Fell
2630 feet
802 m

Allow 5 hours
actual walking time
to Borrowdale by
direct route.
Alternative summit
route allow
8 hours

N
E
W
S

Burnthwaite
farm

WASDALE HEAD

Lunch: If you take the southern face route you could take lunch at the friendly café in Seathwaite. Suggest you telephone them (059 684 293), to check they will be open.

If you take the summit route I suggest you take a packed lunch. The Westmorland Cairn provides a breath-taking stopping-place if the weather makes it practical, otherwise a sheltered spot down by Sty Head Tarn provides a dining-room of rare magnificence.

## Wasdale Head to Sty Head Tarn

**Going:** A long walk up the steep path that crosses the southern face of the magnificent rock and scree pile of Great Gable. A climb of 1200 feet *365 m*. If the weather is good and promises to remain so; and if you have faith in the strength of your legs; and if you are able to do some simple navigation; then you could take the alternative route and visit the summit that provides one of the most exciting views in Lakeland.

The path from Wasdale Head passes behind Burnthwaite Farm and between drystone walls to bridge over Gable Beck.

On Left just beyond bridge, a track rises very steeply to Beck Head Pass between Kirk Fell (Left) and Great Gable (Right). Down this old track, known as Moses' Trod, slate was carried from quarries at Honiston, on its way to Ravenglass port. It gets its name after a quarryman called Moses Rigg who, legend says, was wont to produce illegal whisky up in his quarry hut.

From the bridge the path continues rising steadily and remorselessly to the head of the pass.

Be certain to look back down the valley as you climb. Across valley of Lingmell Beck, on your Right, are dramatic Lingmell Crags. Left of these is the deep cleft of Piers Gill, scene of many climbing accidents. In 1921 a lone climber fell here breaking both ankles. By chance some climbers found him 18 days later, miraculously still alive.

High up to the Left of the path are the crags of The Napes, beloved of climbers.

At the head of the pass (Mountain Rescue first aid kit and stretcher) descend easily to the attractive Sty Head Tarn.

### Great Gable summit alternative:

Ascend very steeply up grass track of Moses' Trod. Below prominent 8 feet *2·5 m* high rock of Moses' Finger, the track bears Left to cross screes, and climbs to the pass of Beck Head at 2040 feet *621 m*. Track disappears on the often boggy plateau, but go forward to take stony track on Right, just before iron posts of old boundary fence. This cairned track scrambles steeply up the north-west ridge, keeping to Left, for about 900 feet *275 m*.

The memorial bronze plaque on the summit rocks was erected in 1924 by the Fell and Rock Climbing Club.

A few yards below the summit is the Westmorland Cairn, marking the best view in Lakeland. Don't miss it.

To locate track down to Sty Head, stand with back to summit memorial plaque and turn to Right. Well-worn track down is steep and stony; take care.

Rejoin main route to Sty Head Tarn.

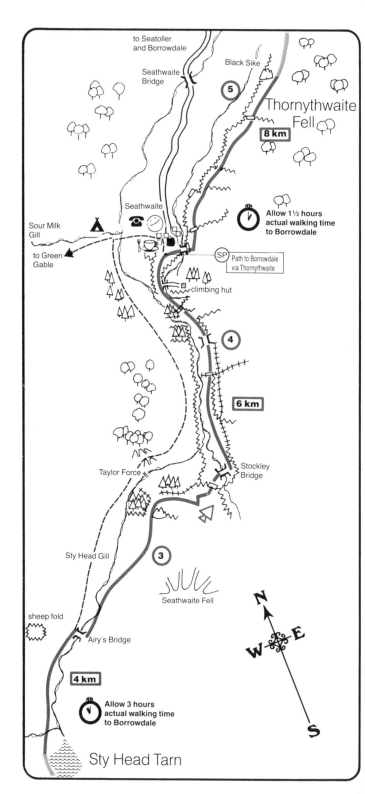

to Seatoller
and Borrowdale

Seathwaite
Bridge

Black Sike

⑤

Thornythwaite
Fell

8 km

Allow 1½ hours
actual walking time
to Borrowdale

Seathwaite

Sour Milk
Gill

to Green
Gable

SP Path to Borrowdale
via Thornythwaite

climbing hut

④

6 km

Taylor Force

Stockley
Bridge

Sty Head Gill

③

Seathwaite Fell

N
W          E
S

sheep fold

Airy's Bridge

4 km

Allow 3 hours
actual walking time
to Borrowdale

Sty Head Tarn

# Sty Head Tarn to Thornythwaite Fell

**Going:** Downhill all the way. A little stony in places but this popular path is easily followed and provides a delightfully relaxed walk after the morning's exertions.

The path from Sty Head Tarn down into Seathwaite has been blazed by thousands of walking boots, and all you need to do is walk and enjoy the wonders of the surroundings.

At Airy's Bridge, cross over to the Right bank of Sty Head Gill.

The track that remains on the Left bank also leads down to Borrowdale and gives the best views of the falling waters of the 100 feet *30 m* Taylor Force, but an awkward spot of scrambling probably results in it being less popular.

The section between the copse at Taylor Force and Stockley Bridge resembles an ancient paved highway of the Incas; the result of the National Trust's attempts to combat massive erosion.

After Stockley Bridge the path levels off and provides an easy stroll to the hamlet of Seathwaite.

In the summer, especially at week-ends, a large proportion of the cars in Lakeland appear to be attempting to park at Seathwaite. This popular starting-point for so many walking expeditions boasts of a mountain rescue post, a public telephone, toilets and a café. The café opens from 10.00 to 18.00 hrs every day except Fridays from Easter to October. Apart from life-giving mugs of tea, you can get substantial snacks like trout and chips!

And next door you can also buy live trout throughout the year!

In 1844 a rain-gauge was installed here and this hamlet of 500 feet *150 m* now has the reputation of being the wettest spot in England. Its average rainfall is 130 inches *330cm*. By comparison Keswick, only 9 miles *14 km* down the dale, claims a mere 51 inches *129 cm*. (London averages 24 inches *61 cm* a year.)

Near here plumbago or graphite was mined in great quantities, and the black lead, known locally as 'wad' resulted in Keswick's fame for lead pencils. Although the local 'wad' ran out in 1880 the pencil industry still thrives in Keswick. Indeed one of the delights of that busy tourist town is the fascinating Pencil Museum there. The first pencil factory opened in 1566, two years before Shakespeare was born. I wonder if he learned to write with a pencil from Cumbria?

As you enter Seathwaite you will see the signposted path to Borrowdale on the Right. Cross a footbridge, through the gate and turn Left. In a few yards go through a second gate on the Left to cross a field by a cairned track. With the wall on your Left, this track goes pleasantly through stiles and gates to provide a delightful pastoral walk down the valley.

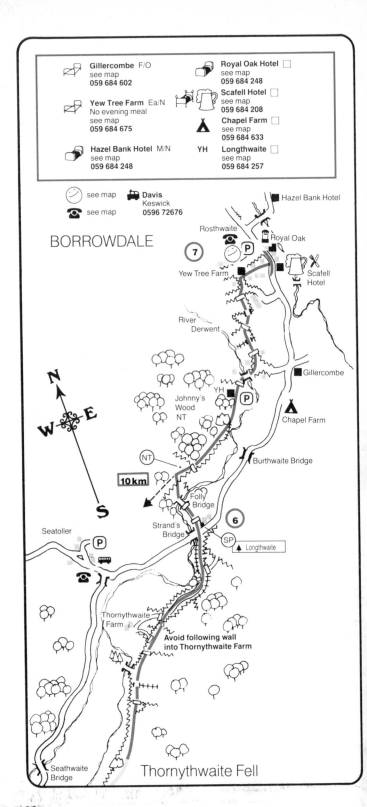

Gillercombe F/O
see map
059 684 602

Yew Tree Farm Ea/N
No evening meal
see map
059 684 675

Hazel Bank Hotel M/N
see map
059 684 248

Royal Oak Hotel ☐
see map
059 684 248

Scafell Hotel ☐
see map
059 684 208

Chapel Farm ☐
see map
059 684 633

YH Longthwaite ☐
see map
059 684 257

see map 🕭

see map ☎

Davis
Keswick
0596 72676

BORROWDALE

Hazel Bank Hotel

Rosthwaite

⑦

Royal Oak

P

Yew Tree Farm

Scafell
Hotel

River
Derwent

Gillercombe

Johnny's
Wood
NT

YH

P

Chapel Farm

N
W E
S

NT

Burthwaite Bridge

10 km

Folly
Bridge

Strand's
Bridge

⑥

SP ▲ Longthwaite

Seatoller

P

☎

Thornythwaite
Farm

Avoid following wall
into Thornythwaite Farm

Seathwaite
Bridge

Thornythwaite Fell

28

# Thornythwaite Fell to Borrowdale

**Going:** A pleasant pastoral stroll into the delights of Borrowdale.

The field path continues, with wall on the Left. Beware that you are not lulled into following path through gateway on the Left, into Thornythwaite Farm.

A stretch of walled farm road follows, and soon reacquaintance is made with Sty Head Gill on Left; however it has now become the River Derwent, gurgling its way to Derwentwater.

Cross with care over the busy Buttermere to Keswick road at Strands Bridge, and continue ahead along track to gated Folly Bridge. Rise up diagonally Right to cross remains of wall and turn Right on track. Enter Johnny's Wood.

Johnny's Wood is owned by the National Trust and is listed as an Area of Special Scientific Interest for its exuberence of ferns, mosses and lichens.

The National Trust advise us that the wood is of special interest to bryologists. Of course!

The path continues to follow the Derwent until just beyond Longthwaite Youth Hostel, where cross the stone bridge on the Right.

Up the lane for a few yards, and at the T junction, turn Left by Castle Lodge, to follow signposted field footpath.

Behind row of grey-slated houses, leave field by gate on to lane, where turn Right and Left. Before Nook Farm turn Right along footpath between houses to emerge on to road at Rosthwaite.

Borrowdale is considered by many to be the most beautiful dale of all Lakeland. Certainly it has thrilled writers, poets and painters ever since Thomas Gray produced his *Journal of a tour in the Lakes* in 1775.

This glaciated valley with its high steep sides is heavily wooded and the magical display of new leaves of every shade of green in the spring, and the breath-taking tapestry of crimsons and gold in the autumn, can stir the soul of all but the dull.

The valley is particularly popular with naturalists. The woods, many in the care of the National Trust, are rich in ferns, lichens and mosses, some of which are only to be found in this valley.

The dale accepts water from all the surrounding hills and is an easy victim to flooding. The inhabitants still talk of the terrible flood of 1966 when roads and bridges were washed away and the valley floor became an extension of Derwentwater.

Sir Hugh Walpole, the celebrated novelist who spent his last days in Borrowdale, would no doubt be amused to see that no less than three establishments in Rosthwaite claim to be the farm featured in his novel, *Rogue Herries.*

The people of Rosthwaite have been housing walking visitors here for many years, and well understand their needs. Not least of these needs is a warm welcome, and that you will find aplenty.

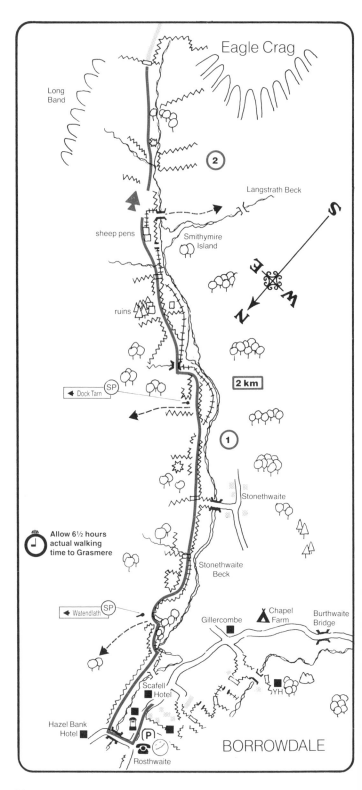

Eagle Crag

Long Band

②

Langstrath Beck

sheep pens

Smithymire Island

ruins

← Dock Tarn SP

2 km

①

Stonethwaite

Allow 6½ hours actual walking time to Grasmere

Stonethwaite Beck

← Watendlath SP

Gillercombe

Chapel Farm

Burthwaite Bridge

YH

Scafell Hotel

Hazel Bank Hotel

P

Rosthwaite

BORROWDALE

30

Lunch: you will need a packed lunch today.

# Borrowdale to Eagle Crag

**Going:** A most attractive walk along the meandering Stonethwaite Beck. After Langstrath Beck this ancient track begins to climb to Eagle Crag.

At the Post Office end of the hamlet of Rosthwaite, turn Right in the direction of Hazel Bank Hotel. Immediately over the stone bridge, turn Right to follow the lane which follows Stonethwaite Beck. This eventually becomes a pleasant field track.

A track off to the Left is to Watendlath, a hamlet in an attractive and remote setting beside a tarn. Much visited by motor-car tourists, and the setting for Sir Hugh Walpole's 1920s best-seller, *Judith Paris.*

Pass by ruins of cottages.

Ahead the great bluff of Eagle Crag dominates the valley.

The Stonethwaite Beck along which our route lies is fed by Greenup Gill ahead, and the Langstrath Beck which comes in from the fine valley opening on the Right.

An important medieval pack-horse route once went up this Langstrath Valley to an important crossroads at 2000 feet *610 m* where trails went off to Wasdale for the port of Whitehaven, to Eskdale for the port of Ravenglass and to Mosedale and Dunnerdale for Furness.

The great Cistercian Priory at Furness, 25 miles *40 km* to the South of here, owned a great deal of property in Wasdale, Eskdale and Borrowdale, and became rich through agriculture, wool and mining. In this valley they used to smelt iron ore on this spit of land, known as Smithymire Island, that lies at the junction of the feeder becks. Farther up Langstrath Valley, the pony track route goes through Ore Gap, a pass at 2575 feet *785 m*, between Bowfell and Esk Pike.

From Langstrath, the path begins to climb quite steeply, so adopt a nice steady pace with a slow rythym, and this will present no problem.

As the path climbs up to the Left of Eagle Crag, this fearsome pile softens to yet another majestic, steep-sided fell.

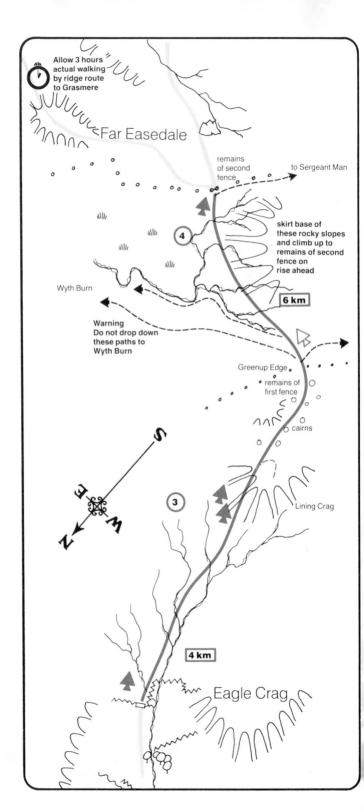

Allow 3 hours actual walking by ridge route to Grasmere

Far Easedale

remains of second fence

to Sergeant Man

skirt base of these rocky slopes and climb up to remains of second fence on rise ahead

4

6 km

Wyth Burn

Warning
Do not drop down these paths to Wyth Burn

Greenup Edge

remains of first fence

cairns

S

E

W

N

3

Lining Crag

4 km

Eagle Crag

# Eagle Crag to Far Easedale

**Going:** The steep path up continues, enlivened by a little scramble up by Lining Crag. At Greenup Edge the path drops down to cross the top of the soggy Wyth Burn basin, and then climbs briefly again to the head of spectacular Far Easedale.

Continue to climb the clear track to the head of the valley, remembering to look back from time to time over Borrowdale and some of the distant giants.

There is a flat green sward at the foot of the forbidding Lining Crag. This usually seems a sensible place to pause and gird oneself for the scramble up the steep, stony, and often wet gully, that climbs up the Left of the crag. At the top, reward yourself by diverting a few paces to the Right, to rest on top of this superb viewpoint. The real hard work of the day has now been done.

Beyond Lining Crag the ground is much less steep, but the path ahead becomes less clear. Follow the cairns which bear gently to the Right until a few rusty posts embedded in rocks mark the line of the old Greenup Edge fence. This is the summit of the 2000 feet *610 m* Greenup Pass.

From this airy and splendid spot the path drops clearly down, at first peaty, becoming increasingly stony. After about 10 minutes the path levels out to traverse the base of the slopes on the Right. Be very alert against following odd tracks that wander off to the Left, across the stream-streaked basin. Hug the bottom of the slopes on the Right.

Ahead a slight rise leads to a second line of rusty posts, which includes a ladder-like stile. Purists climb over the stile, I tend to lean against it breathing heavily!

This is the head of Far Easedale.

Such a grandstand viewpoint seems an ideal place to take lunch. Find a cranny out of the wind and take a well-earned repast. After lunch it is decision time.

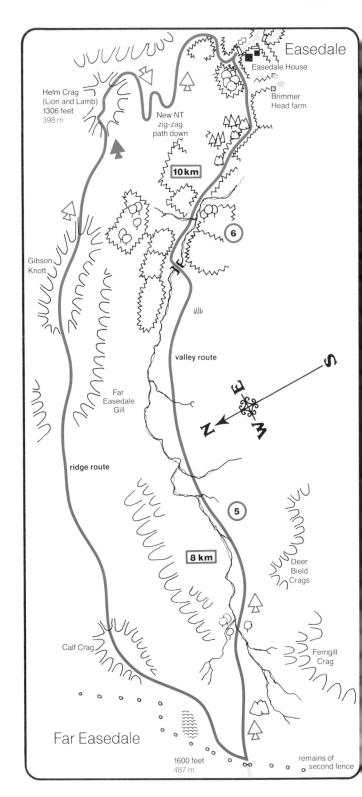

Easedale

Easedale House

Brimmer
Head farm

Helm Crag
(Lion and Lamb)
1306 feet
398 m

New NT
zig-zag
path down

10 km

6

Gibson
Knott

valley route

Far
Easedale
Gill

ridge route

5

8 km

Deer
Bield
Crags

Calf Crag

Ferngill
Crag

Far Easedale

1600 feet
487 m

remains of
second fence

# Far Easedale to Easedale

**Going:** You have a choice. Either take the easily followed path that drops down the valley; in which case you could be sampling the delights of Grasmere within just over 2 hours.

Or you could take advantage of the height which you have worked hard to attain, and follow the fine walk that traverses the 700 feet *213 m* ridge above the valley.

It is an easy walk that will well repay the morning's exertions and will take about an hour longer than the valley route.

**Valley route:**

If you opt for the valley walk, drop down from the ladder stile. The path quickly becomes clear as it follows Easedale Beck down the middle of the valley. No other navigation is necessary until you reach the road at Easedale House. A beautiful relaxing walk.

**Ridge route:**

If the weather is fine, and visibility is good, and you feel that you haven't yet earned the dinner that awaits you, then take to the ridge. You will be well rewarded.

A distinct track goes off to the Left from the ladder stile clearly heading for the Left-hand arm of the valley. On your Left you soon pass a small tarn.

The path rises briefly up over Calf Crag.

I suggest you venture to the Right occasionally to look down into the valley and see the route you might have taken.

Across Gibson Knott at 1379 feet *420 m* the path twists and turns, finally leading down a grassy stretch. The last climb of the day is up to the splendid Helm Crag, at 1299 feet *396 m*, known also as the Lion and the Lamb. This is a fascinating jumble of rocks which you suddenly clear for a glorious view over the village of Grasmere with its attendant lake.

From the summit the considerate National Trust has engineered a fine zigzag path, in places paved against erosion, and this brings you rapidly down to a walled lane where you turn Left and through a gate near Easedale House, and so on to the road to Grasmere.

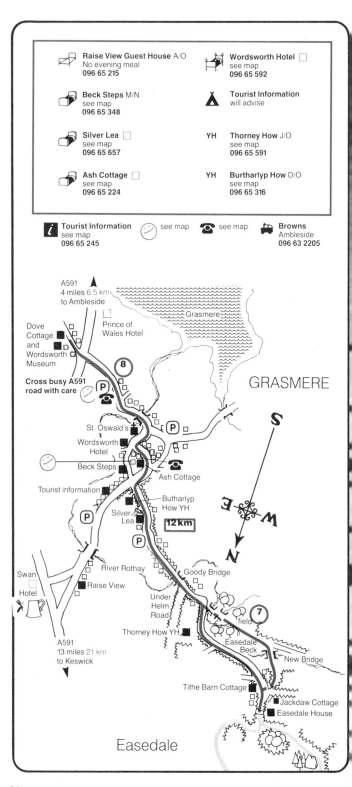

Raise View Guest House A/O
No evening meal
096 65 215

Wordsworth Hotel □
see map
096 65 592

Beck Steps M/N
see map
096 65 348

Tourist Information
will advise

Silver Lea □
see map
096 65 657

YH  Thorney How J/O
see map
096 65 591

Ash Cottage □
see map
096 65 224

YH  Burtharlyp How D/O
see map
096 65 316

*i* Tourist Information
see map
096 65 245

see map

see map

Browns
Ambleside
096 63 2205

A591
4 miles 6.5 km
to Ambleside

Grasmere

Dove
Cottage
and
Wordsworth
Museum

Prince of
Wales Hotel

⑧

GRASMERE

Cross busy A591
road with care

P

St. Oswald's

Wordsworth
Hotel

P

Beck Steps

Ash Cottage

Tourist information

Butharlyp
How YH

12km

P

Silver
Lea

P

Swan
Hotel

River Rothay

Goody Bridge

Raise View

Under
Helm
Road

field

⑦

Thorney How YH

Easedale
Beck

New Bridge

A591
13 miles 21 km
to Keswick

Tithe Barn Cottage

Jackdaw Cottage
Easedale House

Easedale

# Easedale to Grasmere

**Going:** An easy mile into the village of Grasmere.

From here you may put away this guide and follow the road easily into the village. (Note the Goody Bridge over the River Rothay. The Footpath-Touring route out of Grasmere returns to this bridge.)

However, at the beginning, there is an alternative which avoids a ¼ mile *0.4 km* of road walking. This has to be searched for. Just beyond Easedale House and Jackdaw Cottage, on the Right, is a private road. Immediately past this private road, and opposite Tithe Barn Cottage you will see a gate to a narrow walled lane. This leads down to the meadows of Easedale Beck which is crossed by New Bridge. Over the bridge turn Left and follow into trees where two small footbridges recross the beck to lead to the road. Turn Right on the road and so into Grasmere.

Grasmere was described by Wordsworth as 'the loveliest spot that man hath ever known'. And it was William Wordsworth who made Grasmere the best-known village in the Lake District.

On the far edge of the village is the Wordsworth Museum. Adjacent is Dove Cottage, once the 18thC inn, the Dove and Olive Branch, home of Wordsworth during his most productive period. Today it is furnished as it may have been in the poet's day and contains many of his personal items.

I urge you to visit both the museum and Dove Cottage, as they are both well presented. However I suggest that you are there when the museum opens at 09.30 hrs to avoid the crowds of visitors. You are usually free to wander over the cottage, but I recommend you follow one of the lady guides. Their enthusiasm and knowledge of Wordsworth and the family's way of life are as fascinating as the tiny house; their impromptu answers are more revealing than the set commentary. (April to October 09.30 to 17.30 hrs, Sundays 11.00 to 17.30 hrs. March and October 10.00 to 16.30 hrs. Sundays 11.00 to 16.30 hrs. Admission tickets for both museum and cottage available at the museum shop.)

Sturdy looking, 13thC St Oswald's Church resembles those fortified churches that are to be found nearer to the Scottish border. In the chancel is a memorial tablet to Wordsworth who was buried in the south-east corner of the churchyard.

By the church is Sarah Nelson's little shop, once the village school. It sells gingerbread which is baked to a recipe that has been used for 125 years!

Opposite, in the 16thC cottage of Church Stile, the National Trust has a shop and information centre.

The name Grasmere is said to come from the Viking 'Grismere' – the Lake of the Wild Boar. The lake is 1 mile *1.6 km* long, and ½ mile *0.8 km* wide.

The character of Grasmere changes according to the season. In early spring and late autumn it belongs to the inhabitants and earnest-looking walkers. In summer come the cars, the caravans and visitors by the coach-load. But the welcome everywhere is friendly enough, especially for those who have walked here from Ravenglass!

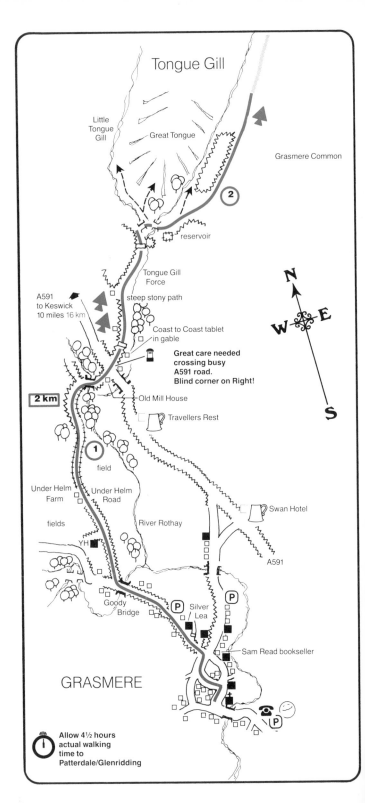

Tongue Gill

Little Tongue Gill

Great Tongue

Grasmere Common

②

reservoir

Tongue Gill Force

A591
to Keswick
10 miles 16 km

steep stony path

Coast to Coast tablet
in gable

**Great care needed
crossing busy
A591 road.
Blind corner on Right!**

N

W E

S

2 km

Old Mill House

Travellers Rest

①

field

Under Helm
Farm

Under Helm
Road

Swan Hotel

fields

River Rothay

A591

YH

P

P

Goody
Bridge

Silver
Lea

Sam Read bookseller

GRASMERE

P

Allow 4½ hours
actual walking
time to
Patterdale/Glenridding

38

Grasmere to Patterdale 1

Lunch: A packed lunch will be required today. The basin of
Grisedale Tarn, after 2$\frac{1}{2}$ hours' walking, makes a delightful setting
when the weather is good. In poor weather shelter from the
elements can be found in the area around Ruthwaite Lodge.

## Grasmere to Tongue Gill

**Going:** A walk along the lane that passes beneath Helm Crag to
join an old stony pack-horse trail that climbs steeply up to the
finger of Great Tongue.

Leave Grasmere opposite the Green, and along Easedale
Road to Goody Bridge. Just beyond the bridge turn Right along
Underhelm Road.

The Thorney How Youth Hostel is on the Left of this lane.

Take the Right fork and over the bridge to cross the very
busy A591 Keswick/Ambleside road. Fast traffic approaches round
a blind bend on your Right, and great caution is necessary when
crossing this road. The route goes up the track opposite, with
white house on the Right. Note the tablet set in the gable-end of
Sandalbeck for the benefit of walkers following A. Wainwright's
celebrated coast-to-coast route.

Down on the Right are the tumbling waters of Tonguegill
Force.

At a gate and stone sheepfold, cross two footbridges to
climb to the Right of the hill which separates Little Tongue Gill
from Tongue Gill. A small reservoir is on the Right.

In fact the old pack-horse track went to the Left of the hill (Great
Tongue,) but you will find this path easier, and in my opinion, just
as scenic and exhilarating. The track up by Tongue Gill is very
clear. Remember to look back at the rock shapes on the top of
Helm Crag. You may even be able to discern the lion crouched
sphinx-like with the lamb before it. Or perhaps you can discover
the group said to resemble an 'old woman playing an organ.' Rock
music perhaps?

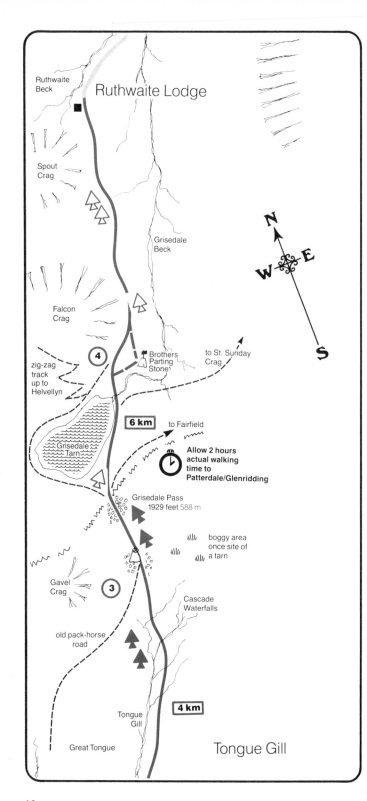

Ruthwaite Beck

Ruthwaite Lodge

Spout Crag

Grisedale Beck

N
W E
S

Falcon Crag

zig-zag track up to Helvellyn

④

Brothers Parting Stone

to St. Sunday Crag

6 km

to Fairfield

Allow 2 hours actual walking time to Patterdale/Glenridding

Grisedale Tarn

Grisedale Pass
1929 feet 588 m

boggy area once site of a tarn

Gavel Crag

③

Cascade Waterfalls

old pack-horse road

4 km

Tongue Gill

Great Tongue

Tongue Gill

# Tongue Gill to Ruthwaite Lodge

**Going:** A steep climb, up a good track, to the pass. Beyond Grisedale Tarn the stony descent can be quite knee-testing in places.

After about half an hour of climbing from the small reservoir, you will come to the water display on the Right known as the Cascades. A sensible place to stop for a few moments to admire the view down the valley.

A cairn-topped boulder, in the centre of the stony path, marks where the old pack-horse trail comes in from the Left.

Just before the final steep climb to the summit of the pass, a boggy depression on the Right looks as if it once housed a small tarn whose outlet became Tongue Gill.

Grisedale Pass, at 1929 feet *588 m* is marked by the remains of a wall. The track drops down to the impressive Grisedale Tarn.

On the far side of the tarn you can usually see stalwarts toiling up the zigzag path that climbs to Dollywagon Pike and the 3118 feet *950 m* summit of Helvellyn.

Legend says that at the bottom of the tarn lie the Crown Jewels of King Dumail of Cumbria. It is said that he cast them here, both to lighten his load and to preserve them, during his retreat from the battle with King Edmund of Northumbria in AD 945.

Cross the Grisedale Beck where it leaves the tarn. The track climbs slightly and bears a little to the Right. It is joined from the Left by the Helvellyn path.

About 30 paces beyond the exit stream look half Right and you should see a small post with a notice-board, fixed in the top of a large rock. Engraved on the stone beneath the notice-board are two verses by Wordsworth, written on this spot to bid farewell to his brother John, who died in a shipwreck in February 1805. The tablet is badly weathered, but if you would know what it says, see Wordsworth's 'Elegiac verses in memory of my brother, John Wordsworth'.

From the tarn basin the path descends into beautiful Grisedale. In places it is stony and steep and you should step with care.

Towering up on the Left are the great craggy slopes of the Helvellyn range.

Water collected from Ruthwaite Cove on the Left joins up with Grisedale Beck.

The climbing hut on the Left was built in 1854 as a shelter for travellers, by the owner of Patterdale Hall. Today it is firmly locked and the key is with a Sheffield climbing club!

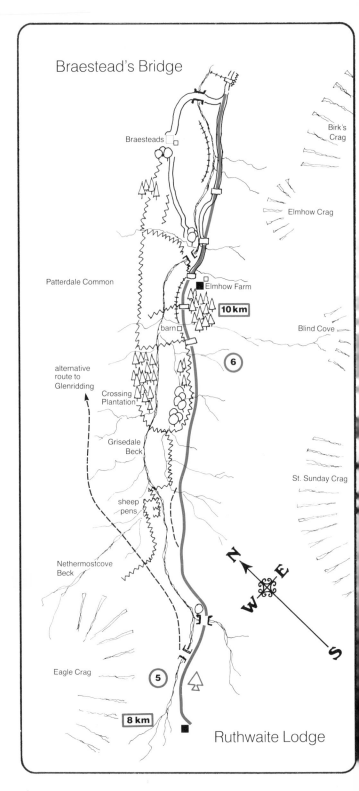

Braestead's Bridge

Birk's Crag

Braesteads

Elmhow Crag

Patterdale Common

Elmhow Farm

10 km

Blind Cove

barn

6

alternative
route to
Glenridding

Crossing
Plantation

Grisedale
Beck

St. Sunday Crag

sheep
pens

Nethermostcove
Beck

N
E
W
S

Eagle Crag

5

8 km

Ruthwaite Lodge

# Ruthwaite Lodge to Braestead's Bridge

**Going:** A gentle downhill walk on an easy track which develops into a farm road.

A relaxing walk down a wide and beautiful valley; a typical Lakeland scene. On the Left are the great slopes of the Helvellyn range, probably England's most climbed mountain. On the opposite side of the valley, the St Sunday Crags tower 2000 feet 600 m above the path. Take your time. This is a walk to savour and remember.

Keep to the Right of Grisedale Beck at the first footbridge.

The wildness of the pass, gradually changes into soft pastureland.

Where a stream comes down from Nethermost Cove, just below Striding Edge, walled sheep-pens offer some kind of shelter when the weather is unkind.

Note the attractive stone bridge on the Left, just beyond Elmhow cottages.

The car track from Elmhow is joined by a tarmac road from Braestead's Bridge.

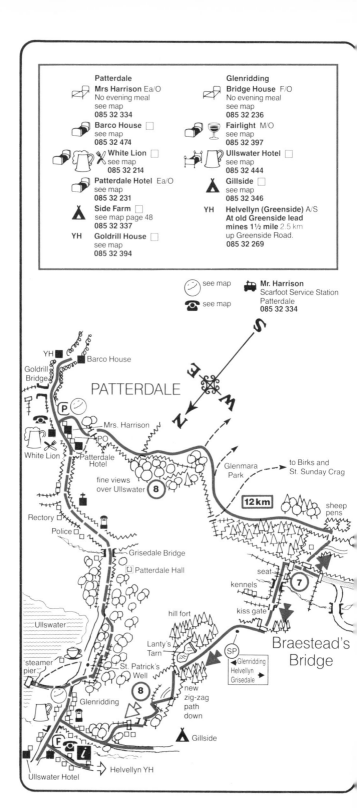

**Patterdale**

**Mrs Harrison** Ea/O
No evening meal
see map
085 32 334

**Barco House** ☐
see map
085 32 474

**White Lion** ☐
see map
085 32 214

**Patterdale Hotel** Ea/O
see map
085 32 231

**Side Farm** ☐
see map page 48
085 32 337

YH **Goldrill House** ☐
see map
085 32 394

**Glenridding**

**Bridge House** F/O
No evening meal
see map
085 32 236

**Fairlight** M/O
see map
085 32 397

**Ullswater Hotel** ☐
see map
085 32 444

**Gillside** ☐
see map
085 32 346

YH **Helvellyn (Greenside)** A/S
**At old Greenside lead
mines 1½ mile** 2.5 km
up Greenside Road.
085 32 269

⊘ see map

☎ see map

**Mr. Harrison**
Scarfoot Service Station
Patterdale
085 32 334

YH
Goldrill Bridge
Barco House
PATTERDALE
Mrs. Harrison
PO
White Lion
Patterdale Hotel
fine views over Ullswater ⑧
Glenmara Park
to Birks and St. Sunday Crag
**12 km**
sheep pens
Rectory
Police
Grisedale Bridge
Patterdale Hall
seat
kennels ⑦
Ullswater
hill fort
kiss gate
Braestead's Bridge
steamer pier
St. Patrick's Well
Lanty's Tarn
SP Glenridding Helvellyn Grisedale
⑧
Glenridding
new zig-zag path down
Gillside
Ullswater Hotel
Helvellyn YH

# Braestead's Bridge to Patterdale

**Going:** It all depends on whether you book accommodation at Patterdale or Glenridding. Patterdale is a magnificently placed hamlet surrounded by the grandest of mountains and set at the foot of beautiful Ullswater. Despite the large number of walkers that head for here, it very largely remains a surprisingly peaceful spot. Glenridding, ¾ mile *1 km* up the road, always seems to be busier with tourists and shoppers.

For those heading for Patterdale there is a pleasant park walk that leads directly into the hamlet.

For Glenridding there is a steep climb up to the site of an ancient hill-fort, followed by a zigzag track that drops down to the village.

Or for either, you could just continue on the tarmac road. Less demanding but much less rewarding.

## For Patterdale

Immediately before a gate across the farm road, go through a gate on the Right, to follow a path by a barn and up to a kissing-gate in a wall. Turn Left in the sheep-pens behind the wall and follow the wall along. The path passes beneath trees and eventually bears Right just before a fence and stile. Follow this pleasant track through Glenmara Park to emerge on to the road in Patterdale. For those staying at the Patterdale Hotel, watch for the short cut to the Left, just beyond a fence.

Patterdale is said to be a corruption of Patrick Dale. There is a popular theory that Saint Patrick once came this way. By the picnic field at Glenridding is Patrick's Well, once said to have healing properties.

The Church of St Patrick owns a delightful 8 bell carillon, and from June to September hymns are played before all of the Sunday services, and also every day when the church is unlocked in the morning, and closed again in the evening.

## For Glenridding

Go through gate across the farm road and immediately turn Left on a track to cross a bridge over Grisedale Beck. Where the track bends to the Right, continue ahead through kissing-gate. Climb steeply up through field to gate in wall ahead. Through gate and turn Right. Follow track which bears Left in front of tree-covered hill-fort. Past reservoir, Lanty's Tarn, on Right. Through gate at end of tarn, a new zigzag path has been engineered to combat erosion. Follow this down into lane. Turn Right into Glenridding.

Glenridding was an important mining town in the 19thC. Mining ceased in the 1960s and the mine was the scene of experiments by the Atomic Energy Authority, to test instruments recording underground nuclear explosions.

Some of the old mine buildings house the Helvellyn Greenside Youth Hostel.

In 1927 the village suffered a disaster when the dam of the mine's reservoir burst without warning. A wall of water swept down destroying houses, but amazingly causing no loss of life. The penninsula of the ferry pier, was formed by the flood debris.

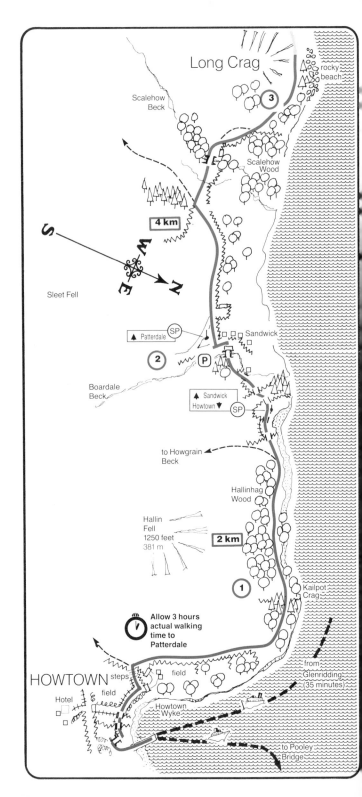

Long Crag

rocky beach

Scalehow Beck

③

Scalehow Wood

4 km

S

W

E

N

Sleet Fell

▲ Patterdale SP

② P

Sandwick

▲ Sandwick
Howtown ▼ SP

Boardale Beck

to Howgrain Beck

Hallinhag Wood

Hallin Fell
1250 feet
381 m

2 km

①

Kailpot Crag

Allow 3 hours
actual walking
time to
Patterdale

from
Glenridding
(35 minutes)

HOWTOWN steps

field

field

Hotel

Howtown Wyke

to Pooley Bridge

# Howtown to Long Crag

It seems a pity to spend time in Lakeland and not to take a journey
on a lake. This suggested excursion not ony includes a venerable
'steamer' cruise on what many consider to be Cumbria's most
glorious stretch of water; it also includes a most delightful lakeside
stroll.

Lunch: If you catch the 11.30 hrs 'steamer' you could consider
using the snack and bar service on board for an early lunch. Better
still, take the Grand Cruise and explore the whole length of this
magnificent 7½ mile *12 km* long lake. Catch the 11.30 hrs service
from Glenridding. Travel to Pooley Bridge but stay on the boat for
the return trip to Howtown. During the voyage take advantage of
the snack and bar service. (Telephone Mr Kirkup, 085 32 502 the
night before to order the special Footpath-Touring snack lunch.)
Arrive at Howtown at 13.00 hrs ready to start walking. Perfect!

Otherwise carry lunch to be taken somewhere on the path. There
are numerous idyllic sites on the way.

The splendidly named Ullswater Navigation & Transit Company
was formed in 1855 to provide a regular steamship service on the
lake. Apart from passengers and goods, the service was originally
charged with transportation of the Royal Mail between Glenridding
and Pooley Bridge. The company owns two handsome launches,
both of which were once steam driven, but now are diesel engine
powered. However, both retain their fine red funnels and are
affectionately referred to as 'steamers'. *Lady of the Lake* was
launched in 1877, and the *Raven* came into service 12 years later.
Both sell sandwiches and have a licensed bar. Apart from the
regular timetable journeys, both craft may be privately chartered for
day or evening excursions.

The main service operates from Easter until the end of
September. There is a restricted service during October. The first
voyage leaves Glenridding Pier at 11.30 hrs arriving at Howtown
about 12.00 hrs. Others at 14.00 hrs and 16.30 hrs. Services are
subject to weather conditions and it might be sensible to check
that all is well. Telephone Glenridding 229, or Kendal 0539 21626.

**Going:** A most beautiful walk. It is an easy path, but do take your
time, and savour every step and every change of view.

From Howtown Pier, turn immediately Right to cross the
footbridge over Fusedale Beck. Follow the bank then turn up to
Left to skirt Waternook Farm. Then follow clear path by edge of
lake, through bracken and ancient woods.

A type of freshwater herring, the skelly, or schelly, is to be found
in the lake. It is known only in two other lakes, Red Tarn and
Haweswater, and is thought to have been isolated here after the
Ice Age. Years ago when the skelly abounded, it was the practice
to sling a net across the water from this bank to Skelly Nab
opposite. The lake also contains perch and trout.

At Sandwich Beach, follow signposts to bear inland across
fields, cross the road in the hamlet, and in a few yards follow wall
on the Right.

At Scalehow Beck, cross the footbridge and follow the wall
to rejoin the lake below Long Crag.

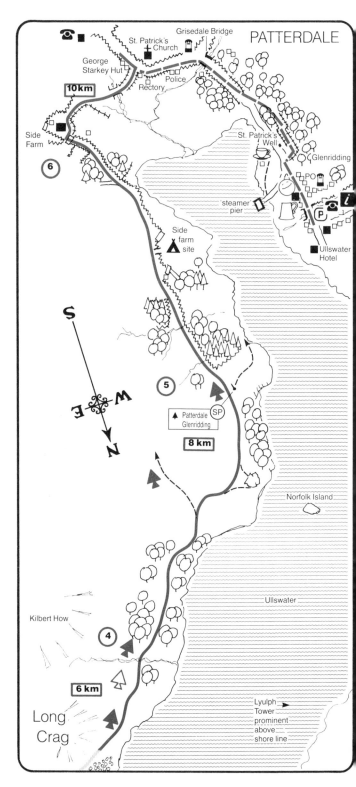

PATTERDALE

Griesdale Bridge

St. Patrick's Church

George Starkey Hut

**10km**

Police

Rectory

Side Farm

(6)

St. Patrick's Well

Glenridding

PO

'steamer' pier

Ullswater Hotel

Side farm site

S

W

E

N

(5)

▲ Patterdale
Glenridding

SP

**8 km**

Norfolk Island

Kilbert How

Ullswater

(4)

**6 km**

Long Crag

Lyulph Tower prominent above shore line

# Long Crag to Patterdale

**Going:** Pleasant path alongside lake becomes a farm track round to Patterdale and Glenridding.

Path continues above a rocky beach with a couple of slight rises.

Where an alternative path climbs up behind Silver Crag, keep to lakeside route.

Ullswater is the second largest of Cumbria's lakes, and is classified as a public highway. A few years ago the peace of the lake was threatened by myriads of water-skiers and the high-pitched whine of power boats. There was opposition to an outright ban on the sport and so a nice Cumbrian compromise was arrived at. Water-skiing is still permitted, but towing craft must not travel faster than 10 miles *16 km* per hour!

In 1961 an attempt was made to turn Ullswater into a reservoir for Manchester Corporation Waterworks and a Parliamentary Bill was promoted. However, the conservationists, aided by the eloquence of Lord Birkitt in the House of Lords, succeeded in quashing the Bill. Lord Birkitt died shortly afterwards and a fell on the western bank is named after him. Later the Water Authority obtained permission to take a limited amount of water from the lake to be fed into their Haweswater Reservoir 5 miles *8 km* away. However it is done very discreetly. The pumping station is underground, and nothing is indicated on the Ordnance Survey maps.

Across the lake can be seen the castellated building of Lyulph's Tower. This striking edifice was built about 1800 as a hunting-lodge by the Duke of Norfolk. It is said to stand on the site of a pele (tower) built by Lyulph, the first Baron of Greystoke. To the Left of the building is Gowbarrow Park, thought to be the area where Mary and William Wordsworth came upon the famous 'host of golden daffodils'. The park also contains Lakeland's most popular waterfall, the 60 foot *18 m* Aira Force. Public subscriptions purchased the estate for the National Trust in 1906.

At the top of a wooded knoll, follow a wall on the Right all the way to Side Farm.

Side Farm opens a little shop on the path from Easter to October offering a restricted but very welcome range of cold drinks and confectionery.

At the farm turn Right on to the field track which leads into Patterdale by the school, and opposite St Patrick's Church.

For Glenridding follow the busy road to the Right but keep to the pavements which switch from side to side. Beyond the lane on the Left to Grisedale, the path goes up into woods a few feet to travel parallel with the road. It returns to the road a few yards beyond St Patrick's Well and opposite the picnic field.

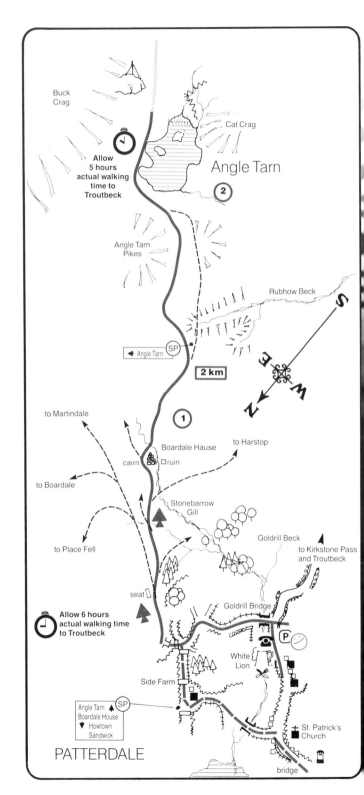

Buck
Crag

Cat Crag

Angle Tarn

② Allow
5 hours
actual walking
time to
Troutbeck

Angle Tarn
Pikes

Rubhow Beck

← Angle Tarn SP

2 km

to Martindale

①

Boardale Hause

to Harstop

cairn 🌳 ▢ruin

to Boardale

Stonebarrow
Gill

to Place Fell

Goldrill Beck

to Kirkstone Pass
and Troutbeck

seat 🪑

Goldrill Bridge

Allow 6 hours
actual walking
time to Troutbeck

White
Lion

P

Side Farm

Angle Tarn SP
Boardale House
▼ Howtown
Sandwick

St. Patrick's
Church

PATTERDALE

bridge

Lunch: A packed lunch will be necessary on this high-level walk.

## Patterdale to Angle Tarn

Important: This is a long and demanding day and an early start is essential.

In reasonable visibility the route is very straightforward and the views immensely rewarding. However, if visibility is likely to be poor because of heavy rain or mist above 2000 feet *600 m*, I suggest you be very wary of this high-level route. Check with the Lakeland Weather Service (telephone 09662 5151).

If prudence suggests a non-walking day, I suggest you treat yourself, and take transport direct to Troutbeck to seek comfort and solace in The Mortal Man, followed by a visit to the superbly presented National Trust Town End Farmhouse (see page 59).

From Easter to September there is a bus service from Patterdale to Troutbeck, operated by the excellent Mountain Goat (telephone 09662 5161). The journey takes half an hour and buses leave from the petrol station opposite the White Lion, at 11.34 hrs, 14.25 hrs, 17.00 hrs and 19.20 hrs. Alternatively Mr Harrison's taxi service will take a full car for a reasonable fee; mention Footpath-Touring.

**Going:** A steady ascent of 1200 feet *366 m* up a good track. In three places care must be taken to take correct path. A fine walk with magnificent views.

Leave Patterdale by the Windermere Road. Just beyond White Lion turn Left to cross Goldrill Bridge. Take Left fork. Where walled road curves to Right, opposite gate to Side Farm, go through gate ahead on to the fells, and take rising track to Right.

Take Right fork near seat and continue to climb steadily.

Remember to look back for fine views over Patterdale.

At level by ruin and cairn, bear Right to cross Stonebarrow Gill and follow rising path.

There are splendid views here over Brothers Water and the adjoining pastures on the valley floor, 1½ miles *2.5 km* away and 1000 feet *300 m* below.

Brothers Water was once the southern end of Ullswater, but mud and gravel, carried down from the fells after an Ice Age, built up to make this separation. Wordsworth suggested in his *A Description of the Scenery of the Lakes in the North of England* that the name may have originally been Broadwater, but was changed after two brothers were drowned in skating accidents.

The path travels below the crags of Angletarn Pikes, 1857 feet *566 m*, to suddenly come upon the perfectly sited Angle Tarn.

Angle Tarn, at 1600 feet *488 m*, is probably the most picturesque of all the mountain tarns, with its interesting shore line and small islands. This delightful bowl makes an ideal spot to rest from exertions, and gather strength for the 1000 feet *300 m*, that lie ahead.

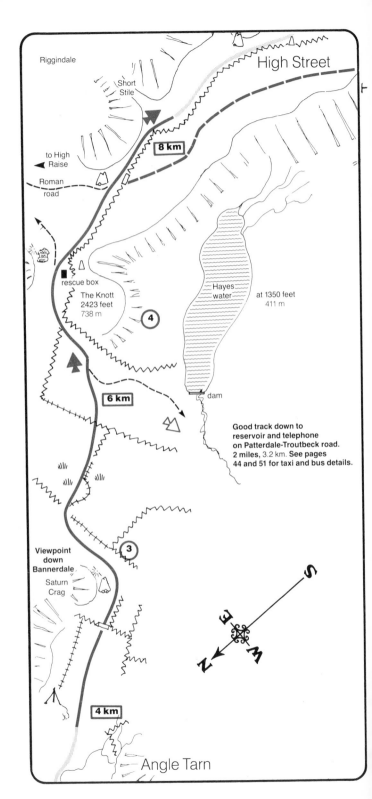

Riggindale

Short
Stile

High Street

8 km

to High
Raise

Roman
road

rescue box

The Knott
2423 feet
738 m

Hayes
water

at 1350 feet
411 m

④

6 km

dam

Good track down to
reservoir and telephone
on Patterdale-Troutbeck road.
2 miles, 3.2 km. See pages
44 and 51 for taxi and bus details.

③

Viewpoint
down
Bannerdale
Saturn
Crag

S

E

W

N

4 km

Angle Tarn

# Angle Tarn to High Street

**Going:** A slow, steady pace will get you to the high point of this ancient, mountain-ridge route. If the weather is kind, all your exertions will be richly rewarded.

The path climbs easily from the Angle Tarn basin.

In about 10 minutes pass through a gate in a wall across the path. A few yards beyond the gate, a low cairn up on a grassy hillock on the Left marks a fine viewpoint down Bannerdale, a bonus easily missed.

The path now drops down to a level, boggy section.

Down in the hollow on the Right lies Hayeswater, now a reservoir supplying water to Penrith, 12 miles *19 km* to the North-East.

There is an escape route from here, down to the reservoir and then to the Patterdale to Troutbeck road; this might be useful if conditions should drastically deteriorate. (See map.)

The path passes beneath the conical hill of The Knott, where an emergency stretcher is housed in a blue box, in the angle of the summit wall.

About 150 paces away to the Left, a diversion offers superb views down the Valley of Rampsgill, with High Raise and the northern stretch of High Street up on the Right.

This valley and Bannerdale lead to Martindale, a private nature reserve, where there is a protected herd of the last wild red deer in England. Keen eyesight and patient scanning are required to spot them, although I have seen them very close to the head of this valley.

From The Knott, follow the wall on the Right.

By a cairn, the Roman road of High Street comes in on the Left.

High Street was almost certainly in use as a prehistoric route, avoiding dense forests and swamps in the valleys, long before the Romans made it an infantry route from their Fort of Galava at Ambleside, to Brocavum Fort at Brougham near Penrith.

The Roman road descends and, in a few yards, passes through the wall on the Right. This ancient route may be taken, with its good views over the Hayeswater Valley. However, by far the best route is to continue on the track ahead, keeping the High Street wall on your Right.

This track leads to the summit of the High Street ridge, and you are urged to deviate over to the Left for tremendous views from the cliff-edges, down Rigginldale, to Haweswater.

Haweswater, the most eastern of the lakes is a reservoir providing water for Manchester. In the 1930s the capacity of the lake was increased by building a 90 feet *28 m* long, and 120 feet *37 m* high dam. This resulted in submerging the village of Mardale Green.

In periods of drought, the water-level drops and visitors flock to see the lanes and ruins of this lost community. The last time this occurred was in the dry summer of 1984.

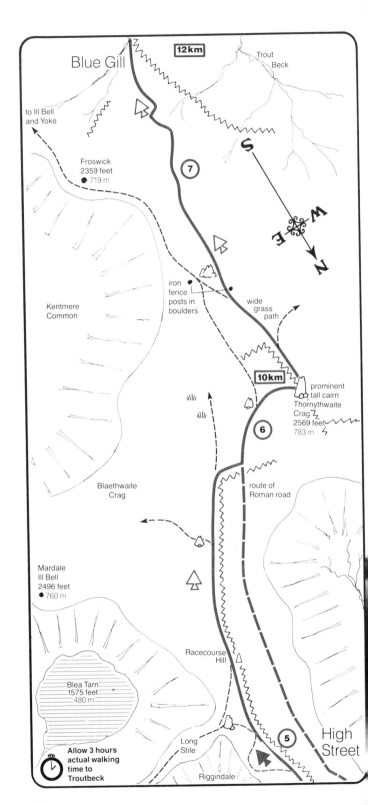

Blue Gill

12km

Trout Beck

to Ill Bell and Yoke

Froswick
2359 feet
● 719 m

⑦

S

W
E
N

iron fence posts in boulders

wide grass path

Kentmere Common

10km

prominent tall cairn
Thornythwaite Crag
2569 feet
783 m

⑥

Blaethwaite Crag

route of Roman road

Mardale Ill Bell
2496 feet
● 760 m

Racecourse Hill

Blea Tarn
1575 feet
480 m

Allow 3 hours actual walking time to Troutbeck

Long Stile

⑤

High Street

Riggindale

# High Street to Blue Gill

**Going:** An exciting section with glorious views from High Street. From Thornythwaite Crag, a less distinct track drops down to Blue Gill.

Continue up to summit of High Street, either along the wall on your Right, or preferably farther over to the Left along the cliff-edges to look down the Rigindale Valley.

The valley is bounded on the Left by Kidsty Pike, and on the Right by the narrow ridge of Long Stile. Both provide popular routes down to Haweswater.

The valley annually becomes the home of nesting Golden Eagles, causing much excitement, and arousing the protective instincts of ornithologists from all over the country.

Keep a look out for the white trigonometry pillar by the High Street wall. Be certain to divert to the cliff-edge here to look down to Blea Tarn, cradled in Mardale Waters Cove.

The trig point marks the summit of High Street, also known as Racecourse Hill. Annual fairs were once held here every July to exchange strayed sheep. Eventually this came to include horse-racing on the wide summit ridge, accompanied by Cumbrian wrestling and the consumption of ale!

Continue with the wall on your Right to the corner. An indistinct track goes ahead, but turn to Right round the corner and turn Left to rejoin the route of the Roman road.

This bears to Right and rises up to the prominent 14 feet *4 m* high cairn on Thornythwaite Crag.

At the cairn, cross the wall to follow the wide grass track going off to the Left.

By the path, on the Right, is a post. A second post (an iron fence support embedded in a boulder) marks the spot where track drops down through rocks. (A track to Left heads for the ridge and summits of Froswick, Ill Bell and Yoke.)

The old Roman route, now an interesting assortment of gullies, hollows and terraces, descends down the valley to meet the corner of a wall that comes across the valley from the Right. Blue Gill comes in on the Left.

Ahead, the hill of The Tongue sits in the centre of the valley like the crown of a sombrero. Our route goes down by Hagg Gill, on the Left of the hill. Trout Beck can be seen snaking along on the Right-hand side. In the far distance you can often catch glimpses of the waters of Windermere.

The valley contains fine examples of the skills of the old drystone-wallers. The wall we join can be seen crossing the floor of the valley and zigzagging up the side of the fell on the Right, to Hart Crag at 1900 feet *580 m*. The craftsmen who built this wall would collect their own local stones, and sleep by the wall at the end of a long day. Food was carried to them, high up in the fells, by their womenfolk.

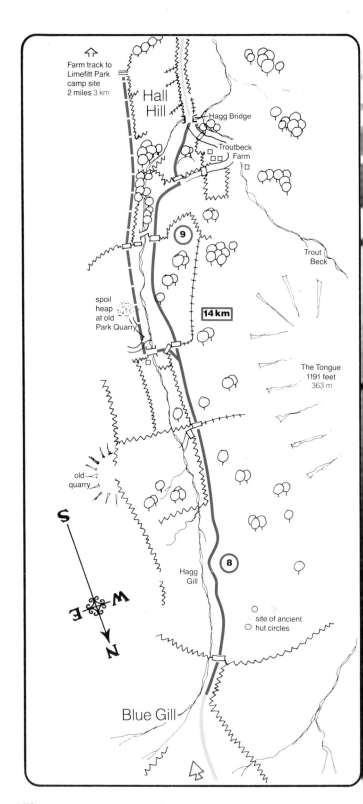

Farm track to
Limefitt Park
camp site
2 miles 3 km

Hall
Hill

Hagg Bridge

Troutbeck
Farm

⑨

Trout
Beck

spoil
heap
at old
Park Quarry

**14 km**

The Tongue
1191 feet
363 m

old
quarry

S

W E

N

Hagg
Gill

⑧

○ site of ancient
○ hut circles

Blue Gill

# Blue Gill to Hall Hill

**Going:** The steep descent soon levels off to follow a pleasant grass path by Hagg Gill. The path shortly becomes a farm lane. Easy, foolproof walking.

Follow wall on your Right down to gate, to enter the water-meadows of Hagg Gill.

This attractive area has not always been so secluded. Many traces of prehistoric stone circles, cairns and huts have been identified here.

The path clearly follows the stream until coming to a wall on the Left. Continue by this wall as track develops into a farm lane.

By a barn on the Left are two gates and a footbridge. This old quarry site marks the beginning of a path along the opposite bank of Hagg Gill leading directly to the campsite at Limefitt Park.

To the Left are the slopes of the 2309 feet *704 m* Yoke.
Up on the Right are the steep slopes of The Tongue.

The name Tongue comes from the Old Norse word *tunga*, meaning a ridge that runs between two valleys which eventually come together.

As the farm lane bears Right, heading for Troutbeck Park Farm, take signposted footpath across the field on left, to Hagg Bridge.

Troutbeck Park is one of the most famous sheep farms in Lakeland. Its 2000 acres *810 hectares* includes the summits of Ill Bell, Froswick and Thornythwaite Crag, and the Roman road down which you have just walked. The farm was acquired by the National Trust in 1944, under the will of Mrs W. Heelis, better known as Beatrix Potter, writer of children's stories.

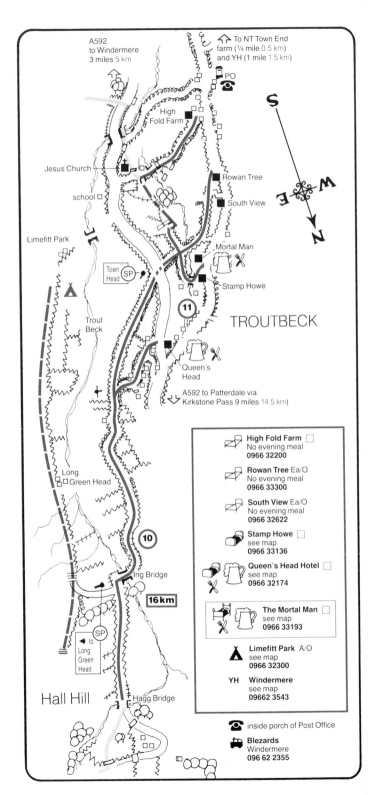

A592
to Windermere
3 miles 5 km

To NT Town End
farm (¼ mile 0.5 km)
and YH (1 mile 1.5 km)

PO

S

High
Fold Farm

Jesus Church

Rowan Tree

South View

school

Limefitt Park

Mortal Man

Town
Head SP

Stamp Howe

11

TROUTBECK

Trout
Beck

Queen's
Head

A592 to Patterdale via
Kirkstone Pass 9 miles 14.5 km)

Long
Green Head

10

Ing Bridge

16 km

SP
to
Long
Green
Head

Hall Hill

Hagg Bridge

High Fold Farm
No evening meal
0966 32200

Rowan Tree Ea/O
No evening meal
0966 33300

South View Ea/O
No evening meal
0966 32622

Stamp Howe
see map
0966 33136

Queen's Head Hotel
see map
0966 32174

The Mortal Man
see map
0966 33193

Limefitt Park  A/O
see map
0966 32300

YH  Windermere
see map
09662 3543

inside porch of Post Office

Blezards
Windermere
096 62 2355

# Hall Hill to Troutbeck

**Going:** A farm lane walk, ending in a walled path that climbs easily up into the village of Troutbeck. A gentle finish to a long and demanding day.

From Hagg Bridge, follow the pleasant farm lane that runs between walled pastures that cover the floor of the valley.

Cross Ing Bridge over Trout Beck.

Are there trout in Trout Beck? The Cumbria Trust for Nature Conservation tells us that there are. The beck flows from its beginnings below Thornythwaite Crag, down the valley and into Windermere.

Just beyond a barn on the Left, the lane turns sharp Right. Take this Right turn for the Queen's Head inn. However, for the centre of the village, take the narrow walled lane ahead that rises up to the A592 road. Cross this busy road with great care, and continue on the lane ahead. Take the first turning to the Right for The Mortal Man and Stamp Howe. Straight ahead for High Fold Farm, Rowan Tree and South View.

Troutbeck is a fascinating village scattered along 1½ miles *2·5 km* of the lower western slopes of the wild and beautiful Valley of Trout Beck. Many of the houses date from the 17thC and there are spinning-galleries and oak-mullioned windows to be found. All are connected by a network of walled paths and tracks.

A warm welcome is offered to Footpath-Tourers by The Mortal Man, an excellent hotel. Parts of the building are thought to be 17thC, and the unusual inn sign was prompted by an innocent verse which greatly amused the Victorians. This historic hotel has offered food and shelter to many famous travellers, including Wordsworth, Coleridge and Southey. Troutbeck's other inn, the Queen's Head, boasts a bar made from a four-poster bed, and offers some good beers, two large fires in the main bar and enormous chip butties – sandwiches filled with French fried potatoes, for those yet to discover this delicacy!

The village has a Post Office which will also sell you a cup of tea. The public telephone is tucked away in an alcove in the porch.

There are several water-troughs in the village, once necessary for the horses before their 4 mile *6.5 km* pull up the unrelenting Kirkstone Pass to the North, highest metalled public road in Lakeland.

At the far end of the village is Town End, a 17thC farmhouse, in the loving care of the National Trust. The house is imaginatively furnished with all the papers, books and furniture gathered by one family over 13 generations. When the house was built in 1626, with its stone mullions and round chimneys, it became the home of George Browne, and it stayed with the family until 1944. Some fine pieces of oak furniture, including a canopied bedstead and a cradle, were carved by members of the family. The house provides the feeling that the family are at present out, but will shortly return. Open 14.00 to 18.00 hrs from April to end October. Closed Saturdays and Mondays. A visit is strongly recommended if you can fit it into your schedule.

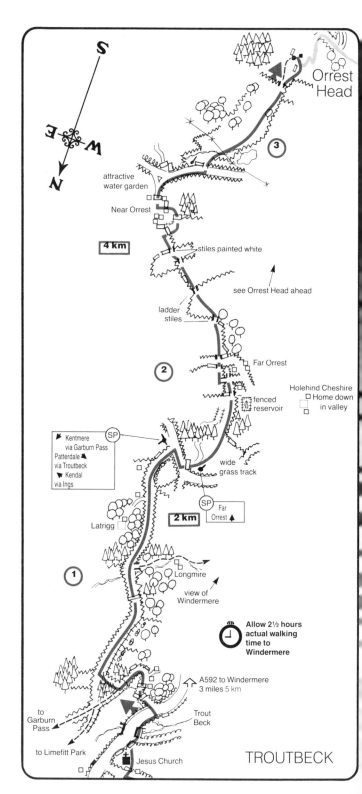

S

E

W

N

Orrest
Head

③

attractive
water garden

Near Orrest

**4 km**

stiles painted white

see Orrest Head ahead

ladder
stiles

Far Orrest

②

Holehind Cheshire
Home down
in valley

fenced
reservoir

SP

↖ Kentmere
via Garburn Pass
Patterdale ◣
via Troutbeck
↘ Kendal
via Ings

wide
grass track

SP  Far
Orrest ▲

**2 km**

Latrigg

①

Longmire

view of
Windermere

Allow 2½ hours
actual walking
time to
Windermere

A592 to Windermere
3 miles 5 km

Trout
Beck

to
Garburn
Pass

to Limefitt Park

Jesus Church

TROUTBECK

Lunch: The short walk to Windermere will take you only about 3 hours even allowing for a coffee stop on Orrest Head, so lunch can be taken in Windermere.

## Troutbeck to Orrest Head

**Going:** A stony, steep path leads up a lane for an easy 1 mile *1.6 km* walk offering splendid views across the valley. Field footpaths continue to the Orrest Head viewpoint.

Leave Troutbeck by one of the many walled paths and visit the church, set away from the village, down on the Patterdale to Windermere Road.

The attractive Jesus Church was rebuilt in 1737 to replace a chapel built here at the end of the 15thC. The mullioned window in the west wall probably dates from the original building. The church has fine oak beams and an oak table thought to be 300 years old. Above the gallery door is a fine coat of arms dated 1737, which includes heraldry of England, Scotland and Ireland, the lilies of France, and the arms of the reigning monarch, George II. The real treasure, however, is the east window. This extraordinarily beautiful example of stained glass was produced by three famous Pre-Raphaelite artists. The main work is by Sir Edward Burne. Assistance was also given by Ford Madox Brown and William Morris who were in the area on a fishing holiday! Do go in if time permits. You have wandered through some of the finest countryside that England has to offer; you presumably have fared reasonably well; and the weather has probably been not too unkind. Perhaps you may think that congratulations or thanks are in order, and this quiet building, on this spot where various emotions have been concentrated for over 500 years, provides a suitable place to ponder.

Turn Right along the pavement of the busy road. Cross the bridge over Trout Beck. In about 100 yards *90 m* the wall on the Right is replaced by a fence. At this point, cross the road with care to enter a narrow walled lane. This very stony lane climbs steeply, past farm buildings. By a clump of fir trees, turn very sharply Right on to a farm lane. The hardest of the walk is now over. Proceed easily along this lane, enjoying the views over the valley on the Right.

After about 20 minutes walking come to a junction with a road. Turn Right here, but proceed with caution as speeding cars attach more importance to avoiding other cars, than dodging slow-moving walkers! Fortunately in 200 yards *180 m*, turn Left into field, on to wide, grass farm track, signposted Far Orrest. Track bears Left, to corner of wall on Right, which is followed to Far Orrest Farm.

Wooden stiles indicate route behind farm buildings. Through gate, to follow wall on Right and cross ladder stile. Bear Left in field to cross second ladder stile. Follow wall on Left, and cross two stiles strikingly painted white. At Near Orrest Farm, follow white arrow that leads you to Right behind buildings, and round Left on to drive. Attractive water gardens lead to road where turn Right.

In 2 minutes turn Left into field, to follow wall on Right that leads up to high point, which is Orrest Head.

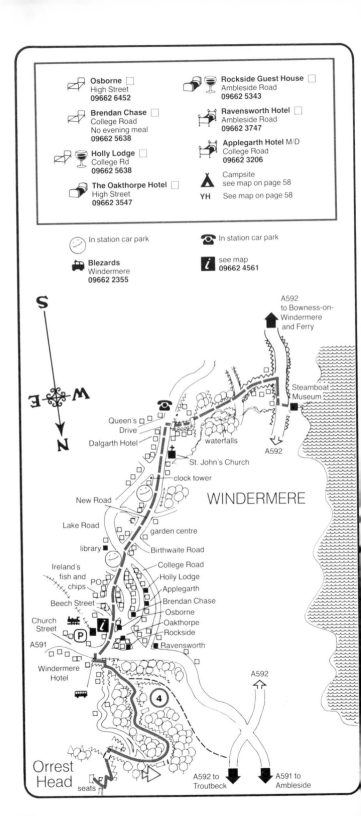

Osborne ☐
High Street
09662 6452

Brendan Chase ☐
College Road
No evening meal
09662 5638

Holly Lodge ☐
College Rd
09662 5638

The Oakthorpe Hotel ☐
High Street
09662 3547

Rockside Guest House ☐
Ambleside Road
09662 5343

Ravensworth Hotel ☐
Ambleside Road
09662 3747

Applegarth Hotel M/D
College Road
09662 3206

Campsite
see map on page 58

YH    See map on page 58

In station car park

In station car park

Blezards
Windermere
09662 2355

*i* see map
09662 4561

S

E · W

N

A592
to Bowness-on-
Windermere
and Ferry

Steamboat
Museum

Queen's
Drive

Dalgarth Hotel

waterfalls

A592

St. John's Church

clock tower

WINDERMERE

New Road

Lake Road

garden centre

library

Birthwaite Road

College Road

Ireland's
fish and
chips

PO

Holly Lodge

Applegarth

Beech Street

Brendan Chase

Osborne

Church
Street

Oakthorpe

Rockside

A591

Ravensworth

Windermere
Hotel

A592

4

A592 to
Troutbeck

A591 to
Ambleside

Orrest
Head    seats

62

# Orrest Head to Windermere

**Going:** From this famous viewpoint, the path drops easily down through woodland, to emerge opposite Windermere Railway Station.

This splendid viewpoint stands at 770 feet *235 m*. An indicator plate identifies the peaks that can be seen to the North and the West. To the East can be seen the Pennines. It is said that on a clear day you can see to Morecambe Bay in the South.

From up here the best view of the 10½ mile *17 km* long Lake Windermere is obtained. However, the Belle Isle tends to look like the southern shore line, when in fact the lake continues for a further 6 miles *10 km*.

The word Orrest is thought to mean 'battlefield'. Certainly it would make a splendid defensive position, and this reasonably peaceful hill perhaps once rang to the noise of a battle.

**Drop down through a kissing-gate and turn Right along by wall. All paths drop down through woods of Elleray Bank to emerge opposite Windermere railway station and Information Office. However the most attractive path is the most westerly as indicated on the map.**

To your Left is the bus stop for Barrow-in-Furness (see page 6).

Windermere is the largest of the Lakeland towns, and resembles a busy seaside resort.

The town took its name from the lake when the railway reached here in 1848. Previously this was the site of the village of Birthwaite. Wordsworth was not at all pleased about the prospect of rail-travellers invading his beloved Lake District, and he opposed the building of the line.

Pleasure-boats of all kinds abound on the lake.

Sealink operates a regular boat service over the length of the lake with its three steamers, *Teal, Tern* and *Swan.* The trip from Ambleside in the North, calling at Bowness, down to Lake Side in the South, takes 1¼ hours. Apart from a short spell at Easter, the service runs from 1 May to end of September. Details from Sealink, Lake Side, Ulverston, Cumbria LA12 8AS (telephone 04483 539).

Bowness Bay Boating Company also run cruises round the lake in motor launches from Easter to October (telephone 09662 3360).

The Windermere Steamboat Museum (see map) has a delightful collection of restored Victorian steam-launches. The 1850 steam-launch *Dolly* was recovered after spending 60 years on the bed of Ullswater, and is the oldest mechanically powered boat in the world. The beautiful steam-launch *Branksome* is extremely elegant, with velvet upholstery, carpets and a marble washbasin, And its steam urn will boil a gallon *4.5 litres* of water in 10 seconds! Open Easter to October, 10.00 to 17.00 hrs (telephone 09662 5565).

The Brockhole National Park Centre has an excellent exhibition telling the story of Lakeland from prehistory to the present day. There is always a full programme of events and it gets very busy, claiming 140,000 visitors a year. Shop and café. Open April to end of October (telephone 09662 5565).

I hope you enjoyed the walk.

# Symbols

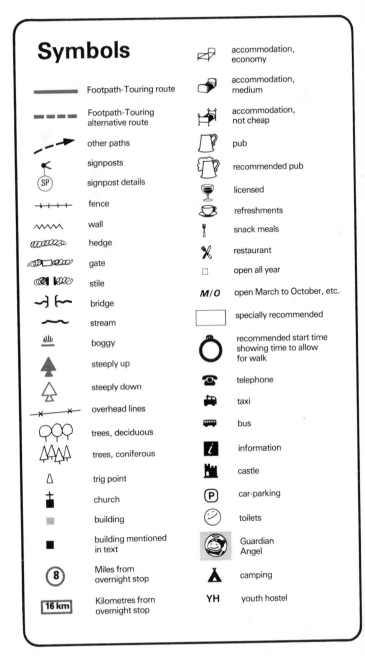

| | |
|---|---|
| ——— | Footpath-Touring route |
| – – – | Footpath-Touring alternative route |
| ↗ | other paths |
| | signposts |
| (SP) | signpost details |
| +++++ | fence |
| ∧∧∧∧ | wall |
| | hedge |
| | gate |
| | stile |
| | bridge |
| | stream |
| | boggy |
| | steeply up |
| | steeply down |
| —×—×— | overhead lines |
| | trees, deciduous |
| | trees, coniferous |
| Δ | trig point |
| | church |
| | building |
| | building mentioned in text |
| (8) | Miles from overnight stop |
| 16 km | Kilometres from overnight stop |

| | |
|---|---|
| | accommodation, economy |
| | accommodation, medium |
| | accommodation, not cheap |
| | pub |
| | recommended pub |
| | licensed |
| | refreshments |
| | snack meals |
| | restaurant |
| □ | open all year |
| *M/O* | open March to October, etc. |
| | specially recommended |
| | recommended start time showing time to allow for walk |
| ☎ | telephone |
| | taxi |
| | bus |
| *i* | information |
| | castle |
| (P) | car-parking |
| | toilets |
| | Guardian Angel |
| | camping |
| YH | youth hostel |

## All about Footpath-Touring

**Further information** on Footpath-Touring, with check-lists suggesting how to keep kit within weight limits and a wealth of other advice and useful tips are included in the publication *Footpath-Touring with Ken Ward, An introduction*, published by Jarrold of Norwich.

0–7117–0145–8 © 1985 Jarrold Colour Publications.
Printed in Great Britain by Jarrold & Sons Ltd, Norwich. 185